THE BIBLE RECAP KNOWII

ACTS

THE SPIRIT AND THE BRIDE

A 10-WEEK BIBLE STUDY
ON GOD AND HIS CHURCH

TARA-LEIGH COBBLE,
GENERAL EDITOR

WRITTEN BY THE D-GROUP THEOLOGY & CURRICULUM TEAM

BETHANYHOUSE
a division of Baker Publishing Group
Minneapolis, Minnesota

Published by Bethany House Publishers
Minneapolis, Minnesota
BethanyHouse.com

Bethany House Publishers is a division of
Baker Publishing Group, Grand Rapids, Michigan

Printed in the United States of America

ISBN 9780764243608 (paper)
ISBN 9781493446919 (ebook)

Library of Congress Cataloging-in-Publication Control Number: 2024046843

The D-Group Theology & Curriculum Team is Laura Buchelt, Liz Suggs, Emily Pickell, Abbey Dane, Kirsten McCloskey, and Tara-Leigh Cobble.

The general editor is represented by Alive Literary Agency, AliveLiterary.com.

Interior design by Nadine Rewa
Cover design by Dan Pitts
Author image from © Meshali Mitchell

Baker Publishing Group publications use paper produced from sustainable forestry practices and postconsumer waste whenever possible.

25 26 27 28 29 30 31 7 6 5 4 3 2 1

CONTENTS

INTRODUCTION

History

The book of Acts was written by Luke, a companion of Paul. Sometimes referred to as The Acts of the Apostles, this letter can be viewed as the second volume of Luke's gospel account; both were written to Theophilus. While the gospel of Luke was about the work and person of Jesus, Acts picks up where the gospel left off to show how the life of Jesus and the indwelling of the Holy Spirit impacted His followers.

Luke is believed to have written Acts in or around AD 63, and the book spans approximately AD 29–62. During this timeframe, we see a handful of believers grow into a multitude of Christ-followers; we witness the establishment of the bride of Christ, His church. It's like watching an acorn growing into an oak tree that produces more acorns, more trees, more acorns . . . until an entire forest is formed!

Resources

Pages 15–19 include additional resources that will serve you well in this study. They include a timeline and maps you'll fill in as you make your way through these stories and journeys of the church's formation.

Persecution

The formation of the church came at a high price under severe persecution from two main sources. First were the same powerful men who put Jesus to death, the Jewish religious leaders and local politicians. Early believers were considered an outlying group of radical Jews until they were first called Christians in Acts 11. The other primary source of persecution was the Roman Empire. In the first century, the Roman Empire controlled large parts of the known world and ruled harshly over anyone suspected of subversion. As you study, take note of which source of persecution was impacting the church in each of the accounts you read.

Context and Purpose

It's important to grasp the context of a Bible passage before making assumptions or applications. As you study the book of Acts, be aware of the difference between the *informative* (descriptive) and the *instructive* (prescriptive). Informative passages are simply accounts of what happened. They describe situations that took place, not commands or promises for believers for all time. On the other hand, instructive passages tell believers how to live, act, or think about a given topic or situation. While there certainly are instructive passages in Acts, there are far more informative passages.

Examples of informative passages are the multiple accounts of disciples being sent to prison, each with unique circumstances and outcomes. So if you read about John and Peter's release from prison in Acts 4 and assume the application to be that God will always free you from difficulty, you will be in for serious disappointment when you encounter Stephen in Acts 7 and James in Acts 12.

The Holy Spirit

As you can tell from the subtitle of this study, we'll spend a lot of time looking at the Holy Spirit and the development of the church. While we don't have time here to unpack the doctrine of the Trinity completely, remember that the Holy Spirit is one of the three members of the Trinity, equal in divinity and unique in responsibility. Acts records a unique incident: the initial indwelling of the Spirit in all believers. To fully understand the way the Holy Spirit works within the church, we must look at the whole of Scripture, not merely this one instance.

A primary role of the Holy Spirit in Acts is to create unity among a diverse group of believers. Sadly, in today's world, defining the role of the Spirit is often a source of disunity among believers. If you're doing this study in a group, make it your aim to let the unity that comes from the Holy Spirit take precedence over any unique views of His roles. For instance, a potentially divisive topic in Acts is the baptism of the Holy Spirit and the "tongues" that followed.

Tongues

There are three primary perspectives on the tongues in Acts 2. The first is that the language that was heard was different from the language being spoken. The believers were speaking in Aramaic but were being heard in Greek, Egyptian, et cetera. The second is that the believers were given a supernatural ability to speak in a language they had not previously known. For example, an uneducated Galilean fisherman who only spoke Aramaic suddenly spoke and understood Greek. The third view is that the tongues are a heavenly language that is unintelligible to humans. Since Acts specifically says people were hearing the gospel in their own language, it's clear that this third explanation is not what is meant by *tongues* in Acts.

Regardless of your local congregation's view of the baptism of the Holy Spirit or tongues in today's context, it's clear that in Acts it was a sign of the working of the Holy Spirit for the expansion of the gospel.

The Bride of Christ

Throughout the New Testament, the church is known as the bride of Christ. The indwelling of the Holy Spirit moved passionate followers of Jesus to turn the world upside down with a message of hope and to establish the bride. For Christ-followers, studying the book of Acts is like watching a documentary about the establishment of our faith via God's work through men and women who sacrificed for us to know Jesus.

HOW TO USE THIS STUDY

While Bible study is vital to the Christian walk, a well-rounded spiritual life comes from engaging with other spiritual disciplines as well. This study is designed not only to equip you with greater knowledge and theological depth, but to help you engage in other formative practices that will create a fuller, more fulfilling relationship with Jesus. We want to see you thrive in every area of your life with God!

Content and Questions

In each of the ten weeks of this study, the teaching and questions are divided into six days, but feel free to do it all at once if that's more manageable for your schedule. If you choose to complete each week's study in one sitting (especially if that time occurs later in the study week), keep in mind that there are aspects you will want to be mindful of each day: the daily Bible reading, Scripture memorization, and the weekly challenge. Those are best attended to throughout the week.

Daily Bible Reading

The daily Bible reading corresponds to our study. It will take an average of three minutes per day to simply read (not study) the text. If you're an auditory learner, you may prefer to listen to an audio version of these Bible chapters.

Even if you decide to do the week's content and questions in one sitting, we still encourage you to make the daily Bible reading a part of your regular daily rhythm. Establishing a habit of reading the Word every day will help fortify your faith and create greater connection with God.

If you decide to break the study up into the six allotted days each week, your daily Bible reading will align with your study. Days 1–5 will follow our study of Acts, Day 6 features a psalm that corresponds to our reading, and Day 7 serves as a catch-up day in case you fall behind.

Scripture Memorization

Memorizing Scripture isn't busywork! It's an important part of hiding God's Word in our hearts (Psalm 119:11). Our memorization passage—Acts 10:34–45—focuses on the importance of sharing the gospel with all people. We encourage you to practice it cumulatively—that is, *add* to what you're practicing each week instead of *replacing* it. We quote the English Standard Version (and some of our resources are in that translation as well), but feel free to memorize it in whatever translation you prefer. We suggest working on each week's verse(s) throughout the week, not just at the last minute. We've provided some free tools to help you with this, including a weekly verse song: MyDGroup.org/Resources/Acts.

Weekly Challenge

This is our practical response to what we've learned each week. We want to be "doers of the word, and not hearers only" (James 1:22). You'll find a variety of challenges, and we encourage you to lean into them all—especially the ones you find *most* challenging! This will help strengthen your spiritual muscles and encourage you in your faith. As with the memory verse, you'll want to begin this practice earlier in the week, especially because some weekly challenges include things to do each day of the week (e.g., prayers, journaling, etc.).

Resources

This is a Scripture-heavy study, and you'll find yourself looking up passages often. If you're new to studying Scripture, this will be a great way to dig in and sharpen your skills! You will feel more equipped and less intimidated as you move through each chapter. Some questions may ask you to refer to a Bible dictionary, commentary, or Greek or Hebrew lexicon, but you don't need to purchase those tools. There are lots of free options available online. We've linked to some of our favorite tools—plus additional resources such as podcasts, articles, and apps—at MyDGroup.org/Resources/Acts.

Groups

Because each week has a lot of questions in the content, we offer the following recommendation for those who plan to discuss the study in a weekly group meeting. As each member is doing their homework, we suggest they mark their favorite items with a star and mark any confusing items with a question mark. This serves as preparation for the group discussion and helps direct the conversation in beneficial ways. Group leaders, please note the starred prompts in each chapter; we've highlighted these for you as topics you may find helpful to prioritize in group discussions.

WHOLE-BOOK RESOURCES

Maps

Journey Map One

Acts 13:4–14:28

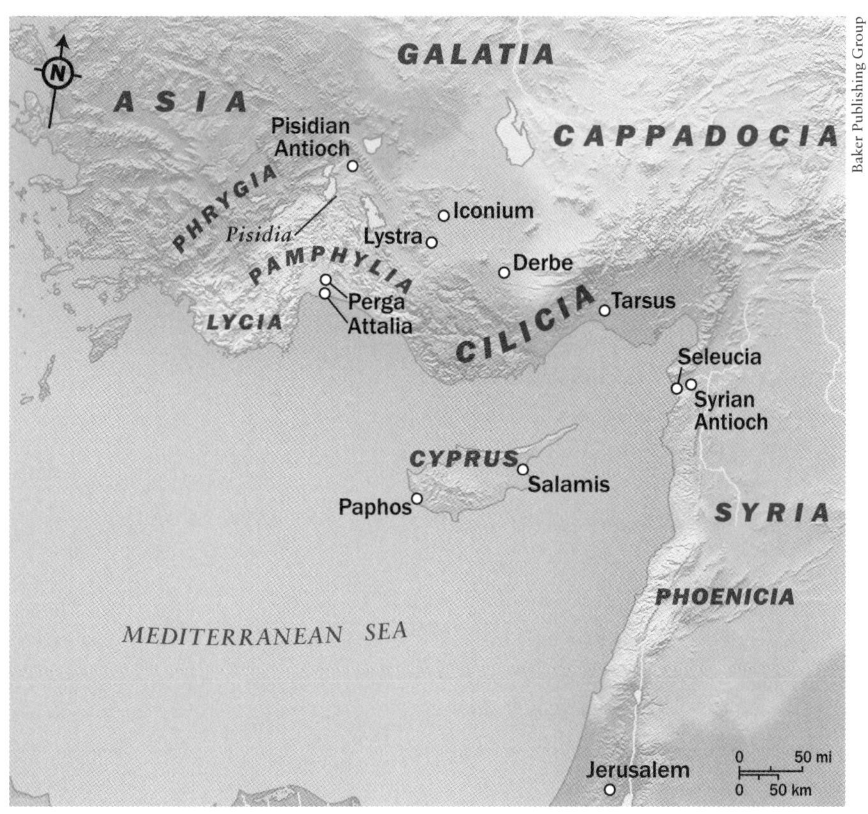

Paul's First Missionary Journey

Journey Map Two

Acts 15:39–18:22

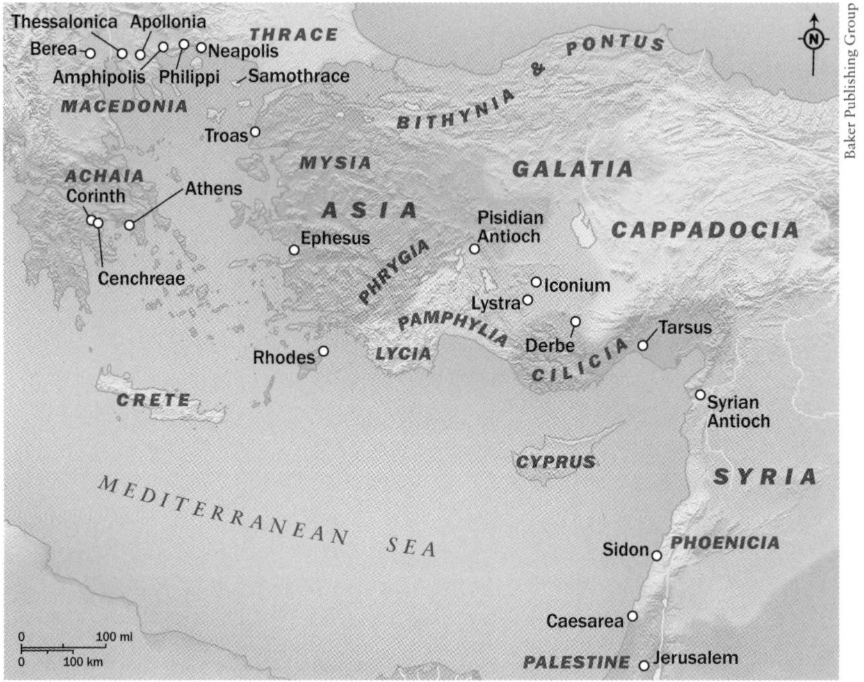

Paul's Second Missionary Journey

Journey Map Three

Acts 18:22–21:17

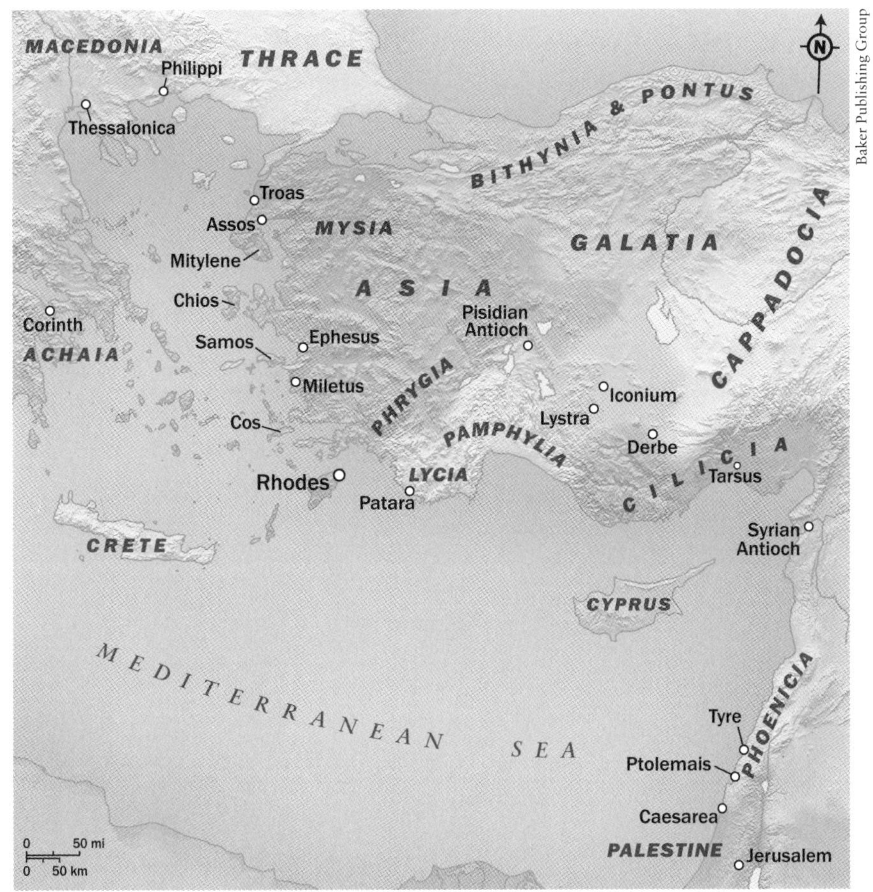

Paul's Third Missionary Journey

Timeline of the Early Church

As you study the book of Acts, you'll fill in this timeline.* At some point, you may wonder, *If Jesus was around thirty when He began His ministry and thirty-three when He died, then shouldn't these years be later?* Despite what our global calendar leads us to believe, Jesus was likely born between 6 and 4 BC, when Herod was king of Judea (Matthew 2:1), when Quirinius was governor of Syria (Luke 2:2), and when Caesar Augustus decreed a census (Luke 2:1). The Gregorian calendar, which the Catholic church instituted in October 1582, inadvertently misdated the year of Christ's birth. This timeline starts after Jesus's resurrection, which was likely around the year AD 29. The dates in the timeline are approximate.

Event	Reference	Approximate Year (AD)
	Acts 2:1–13	
	Acts 2:40–47	
	Acts 4:1–22; 5:21–42; 7:1–60	
First Summary Update on the Growth of the Church		35
	Acts 8:4–13	
	Acts 9:1–9	
Second Summary Update on the Growth of the Church		36
	Acts 10:1–48	40
Matthew's Gospel Written	Matthew	43
James Written	James	45
Third Summary Update on the Growth of the Church		46
	Acts 13:4–14:28	
	Acts 15:6–35	
	Acts 15:39–18:22	
Fourth Summary Update on the Growth of the Church		52

*The Chronology of Acts and the Epistles chart was retrieved from Blue Letter Bible and adapted to include additional timeline information. In the following pages, the † symbol indicates where we have substituted Blue Letter Bible's date(s) with date(s) based on our own study of Bible history.

Event	Reference	Approximate Year (AD)
1 Thessalonians Written	1 Thessalonians	52
2 Thessalonians Written	2 Thessalonians	53
	Acts 18:23–21:17	54
Fifth Summary Update on the Growth of the Church		55
1 Corinthians Written	1 Corinthians	57
Galatians Written	Galatians	57
2 Corinthians Written	2 Corinthians	58
Romans Written	Romans	58
	Acts 21:26–22:29	
	Acts 23:23–26:32	
Luke's Gospel Written	Luke	59
	Acts 27:1–2	
	Acts 28:11–16a	
Final Summary Update on the Growth of the Church		62
Ephesians Written	Ephesians	62
Philippians Written	Philippians	62
Colossians Written	Colossians	62
Philemon Written	Philemon	62
1 Peter Written	1 Peter	63
	Acts	63
Mark's Gospel Written	Mark	64
John's Gospel Written	John	85

WEEK 1

Acts 1–3

Approximate Year: AD 29†

> **Scripture to Memorize**
>
> Peter opened his mouth and said: "Truly I understand that God shows no partiality, but in every nation anyone who fears him and does what is right is acceptable to him."
>
> Acts 10:34–35

Note: If you haven't yet read How to Use This Study on pages 11–13, please do that before continuing. It will provide you with a proper framework and helpful tools.

DAILY BIBLE READING

Day 1: Acts 1:1–11

Day 2: Acts 1:12–26

Day 3: Acts 2:1–13

Day 4: Acts 2:14–47

Day 5: Acts 3

Day 6: Psalm 133

Day 7: Catch-Up Day

Corresponds to Day 320 of *The Bible Recap*.

WEEKLY CHALLENGE

See page 44 for more information.

DAY 1

Acts 1:1–11

 READ ACTS 1:1–11

Review 1:1–3.

Theophilus means "lover of God," so while Luke may have written Acts with one specific person in mind, some theologians believe his intended audience was broader—perhaps even all believers. Even if Luke didn't realize he was writing *to* us, God inspired him to write *for* us. About two thousand years ago, Luke recorded this detailed account of the descent of the Holy Spirit and the birth of the church. Millennia later, Acts still serves to guide and encourage the church.

1. Toward the end of your timeline (page 19), write that Luke wrote the book of Acts in approximately AD 63.

Before we dig into Luke's second volume, let's remind ourselves how volume one ended. (And if you're wondering what that means, we see you, skipper of introductions. Pause and read it now.)

2. **Read Luke 24:45–53.** How did volume one end?

Luke began Acts post-resurrection and pre-ascension. For forty days after Jesus's resurrection, He stayed with His disciples and prepared them to be His witnesses. He spoke specifically about the kingdom of God, which He ushered in and which will come in its fullness when He returns.

3. **Review 1:4–5.** What did Jesus tell the disciples to wait for in Jerusalem? (Hold on to this; we'll study it more in the days ahead.)

4. **Review 1:6–8.** What did the disciples ask Jesus to do in 1:6?

Throughout Israel's history, God's people had waited for a Messiah who would be a powerful military leader, giving them victory over their oppressors. Jesus's disciples voiced what many of His early Jewish followers would've believed about Him: that He came to save them from the iron-fisted rule of the Roman Empire. And while Jesus could've overthrown every kingdom in the world with a single word, He came to do so much more.

Jesus didn't rebuke His disciples for their desire; the restoration of Israel was—and is—a good desire. The disciples' desire wasn't wrong; *it was just too small.* God's plans were—and are—so much bigger than defeating the Roman Empire.

We've all wanted something good that God didn't give us. When God says no, He may bless you with an understanding of why that was His best and kindest answer. Or you may never learn His reason on this side of eternity. Every time God says no, especially to a good desire, it's for

His glory and our good. And with that no, we have an opportunity to grow in our faith.

★ 5. If you have a good desire that remains unfulfilled, write a prayer surrendering it to God's will. Or if you've seen how His no to a good desire was His best answer, write a prayer of thanksgiving.*

★ 6. In 1:8, what did Jesus tell His disciples they were going to do? **Look up *witness* in a Greek lexicon.** Count how many times it's used in the book of Acts.

Review 1:9.

In Luke 24:51, Jesus's ascension into heaven was briefly described. In Luke 1:9, Luke gives us more detail about the miraculous event. The ascension reminds us that Jesus is fully God forever and fully man forever. Jesus had—and has—a physical body. And one day, He will return to earth in His physical body, and on that glorious day, all things will be made new.

* Starred prompts are specifically designed to be useful for group discussion.

7. **Review 1:10–11.** Then fill in the blanks below.

> While they were gazing into heaven as he went, behold, two men stood by them in white robes, and said, "Men of Galilee, why do you _____ _____ _____ _____? This Jesus, who was taken up from you into heaven, _____ _____ _____ _____ _____ _____ as you saw him go into heaven."

Can you imagine the scene? It's highly likely the disciples weren't yet over the shock that Jesus had resurrected from the dead six weeks earlier. Then, after spending forty days talking about the coming reign of the kingdom of God, the disciples watched as Jesus was lifted off the ground and carried up out of their sight in a cloud. It's safe to assume they had their eyes locked on the sky, perhaps feeling grief, disbelief, awe, or worship. Then two angels showed up and asked them what they were staring at.

The angels gave the disciples some reassurance—He's coming back!—and then sent them on their way. The disciples were to be ready for Jesus's return, but in the meantime, there was work to be done.

Two thousand years later, we can read Acts 1:11 with the same reassurance—He's coming back!—and with the same conviction. We are to be ready for Jesus's return, but in the meantime, there's work to be done.

DAY 2

Acts 1:12–26

 READ ACTS 1:12–26

Review 1:12–15.

Using the map below, find and mark the following places: Mount Olives, the upper room, the temple.

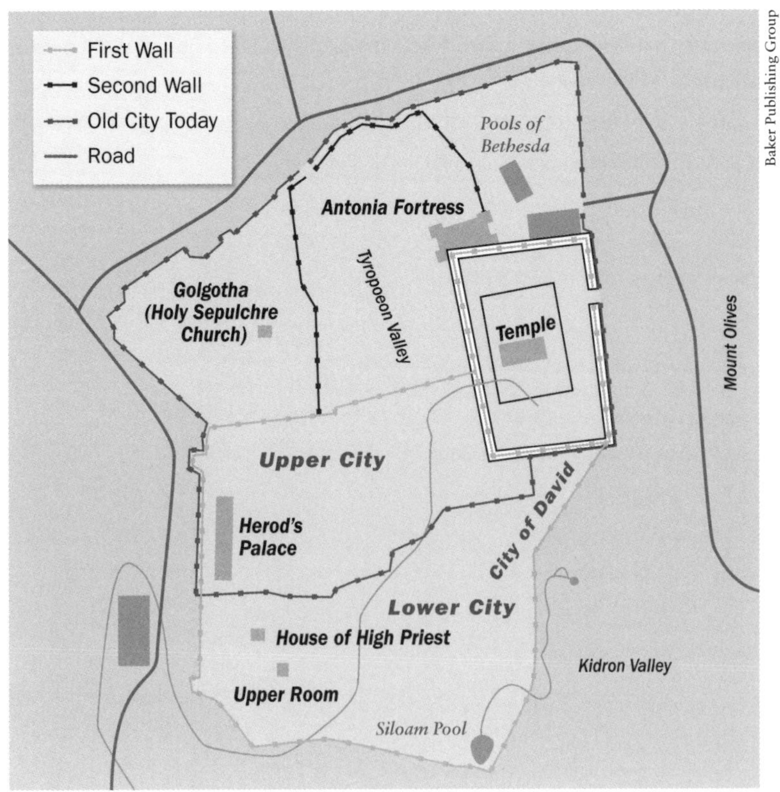

Jerusalem

God gave His people the Sabbath as a day of rest, but Jewish leaders made excessively strict rules about *how* they were supposed to rest. The leaders prohibited work in thirty-nine categories, forbidding things like carrying, writing, and knotting. And they limited what could be done in other categories; on the Sabbath, Jews were allowed to walk a maximum distance of two thousand cubits (a little more than half a mile). After Jesus's ascension, the disciples returned to Jerusalem, which was a Sabbath day's journey away from Mount Olives.

1. Why did the disciples go to Jerusalem after Jesus's ascension?

2. According to 1:15, how many believers were gathered at the time?

The gospel of Luke reveals that women were vital in the ministry of Jesus. Most texts written in the first century referred to women by their relationship to men: wives or daughters. But Luke also named them for their role in God's kingdom—both as disciples and ministers of the gospel. In this scene, not only did Luke note the participation of the women, but he also mentioned Jesus's brothers.

★ 3. **Read John 7:5.** How had Jesus's brothers changed between the writing of this verse and Luke's writing of Acts?

Review 1:16–17.

★ 4. According to 1:16, who inspired David to write prophecy?

"All Scripture is breathed out by God" (2 Timothy 3:16), which means every single word in the Bible is not only inspired but *given directly* by God. God wrote the Bible using the hands and mouths of the men He chose for this work. Praise God for the marvelous gift of His Word that makes us "complete, equipped for every good work" (2 Timothy 3:17).

Review 1:18–20.

If you're familiar with Matthew's account of Judas's death (Matthew 27:3–10), Luke's account may leave you with some questions. The two passages aren't contradictory, but different pieces of the same puzzle. Even though the chief priests purchased the field, they bought it with the silver pieces Judas received in exchange for betraying Jesus. And after Judas hanged himself, the branch that held his body probably broke, causing his body to fall and burst open.

Peter pointed out that these events fulfilled both Psalm 69:25 and Psalm 109:8. In Judas's betrayal and death, both the will of man and the sovereignty of God are on full display. Judas sinned and was held accountable for it. And everything that happened on the night Jesus was betrayed was already accounted for in God's sovereign will.

5. **Use a Bible dictionary to look up *disciple* and *apostle*.** What's the difference?

Disciple	
Apostle	

Judas was one of Jesus's original twelve apostles, and he needed to be replaced to fulfill the prophecy Peter quoted. There would be twelve apostles as a parallel to the twelve tribes of Israel in the Old Testament. Additional apostles would be named in the future, but not counted among the original twelve.

Review 1:21–22.

6. What two requirements were listed for Judas's replacement?

-
-

Two men were nominated for the role: Matthias and Joseph (who was also known as Barsabbas and as Justus).

7. Summarize their prayer from 1:24–25 using the questions below.

- What does God know?
- Who chose Judas's replacement?

The apostles' next step might seem shocking: They cast lots. At the time, it was common practice; marked stones were placed in a pot and shaken out. Sometimes, casting lots was used to gamble, but sometimes, it was used to make decisions. God had revealed His will to His people in this way before: when they divided the promised land (Joshua 18:6–10) and when they determined the division of priests (1 Chronicles 24:1–5).

In the introduction to this study, we mentioned that much of what we see in Acts is *descriptive*; that is, it offers information about how God worked at that particular time, in that particular situation. This is one of those instances. This practice isn't a prescriptive instruction about how to discern God's will. After all, believers today have two things the apostles on that day didn't: the complete Word of God and the Holy Spirit.

God, who knows the hearts of all, had chosen His twelfth apostle: Matthias.

DAY 3

Acts 2:1–13

READ ACTS 2:1–13

When the 120 believers gathered, Luke wrote that they "with one accord were devoting themselves to prayer" (1:14). The believers were described by their unity.

Fifty days after the Passover each year, Jews celebrate Pentecost, also called Shavuot. Also called the Feast of Weeks, Pentecost was a festival of thanksgiving for the firstfruits of the wheat harvest. During this annual celebration, Jews from all across the region journeyed to Jerusalem, bringing with them their various cultures and languages.

That particular Pentecost would indeed be a celebration, just not the kind they were expecting.

1. Update your timeline (page 18) to record that the Pentecost when the Holy Spirit descended occurred in the year 29†.

In Genesis, God gave the command to fill the earth. But some people had other ideas. They built a tower to honor themselves in the middle of a city where they thought they would all live together.

2. **Read Genesis 11:6–9.** What happened as a result of their disobedience?

For generations after this, they lived in various regions, speaking various languages. During a festival like Pentecost, it wouldn't be uncommon to hear a different language spoken by each group that passed by.

Review Acts 2:2–4.

3. How did Luke describe the series of supernatural events that happened next?

Sounded like	
Filled	
Appeared like	
Rested on	

4. What happened when the Holy Spirit filled the believers?

5. **Use a lexicon to look up *tongues* (2:4).** What's the Greek word? What does it mean?

At the Tower of Babel, God divided the people's languages and dispersed them. With the descent of the Holy Spirit, He unified them via another unique and miraculous event.

Review 2:5–11.

★ 6. What's true about the tongues spoken at Pentecost?

A. They were secret prayer languages given to each speaker.
B. They were understood only by the angels and the speakers.
C. They were the native languages of God's dispersed people, each understood individually by the visitors to Jerusalem in their own languages.

★ 7. Which three verses in this section support your answer?

God made the believers able to be understood in foreign languages—despite the fact that they were speaking in their own language—so that the mighty works of God would be shared. Can you imagine the absolute shock and delight this produced among the believers? A supernatural unifying voice, able to be understood by all who believed!

It's worth noting that not everyone present that day believed. Some were openly hostile and mocked what they saw. They claimed those who experienced it were drunk. Signs, wonders, and even miracles aren't enough to convince the hearts that God has not softened.

In the beginning, God the Father created humankind in His image, to live in right relationship with Him and thus with each other. Because of our sin, we broke that relationship. To restore the relationship, God the Son came to live with His people. And to sustain and fulfill that relationship, God the Spirit came to live *within* His people. This is evidence of the new covenant, which will last until the day Jesus returns.

This was why Jesus told His disciples to wait in Jerusalem. This was the promise of God. The time had come for the second person of the Trinity to return to heaven, but the third person of the Trinity had come to stay. He would equip the believers with wisdom, enable them to do God's will, and empower them to minister effectively. And until Jesus returns, *the Spirit will continue to do all this and more.*

8. Match the following passages with ways the Holy Spirit works.

Passage	Way the Holy Spirit works
1 John 4:4	The Spirit guides believers in truth
John 16:8–9	The Spirit fills believers with hope
John 16:13	The Spirit regenerates and renews believers
Titus 3:5	The Spirit convicts the world of sin
Romans 5:5	The Spirit overcomes the world

★ 9. How have you seen the Holy Spirit work in your life?

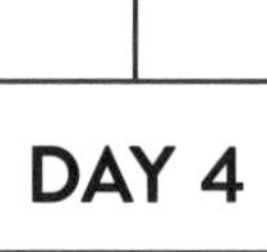

DAY 4

Acts 2:14–47

READ ACTS 2:14–47

After Peter reassured the mockers in the crowd that no one was drunk at nine in the morning, he preached the first of a series of sermons recorded in Acts. Though we have time in this study to go into only a few key points, entire books could delve into the depth and significance of this Spirit-given sermon. We'll focus on three main themes: the fulfillment of Scripture, the sovereignty of God, and the call to repentance.

Review 2:14–21.

Do you remember proofs from your high school geometry class? They're a way to reach a conclusion using agreed-upon facts to prove your steps. Here, Peter explained how prophecy had been fulfilled by systematically going through Old Testament texts—prophecies that were agreed upon as fact by these devout Jews—and explaining how Jesus fulfilled them.

1. Match the following Old Testament references with the prophecy that Jesus fulfilled.

Joel 2:28–32	The Lord makes His enemies a footstool
Psalm 16:8–11	Everyone who calls on the name of the Lord will be saved
Psalm 110:1	The Lord will make me full of gladness with His presence

Peter clearly understood the importance of memorizing Scripture. He probably didn't know when or why he would need to recall the words of Joel, but when the time came, the Spirit brought the words to Peter's mind. This is something the Spirit still does today. Memorize God's Word, and watch how the Spirit blesses your efforts!

2. **Review 2:22–36.** According to 2:23, how was Jesus delivered to His death?

A. It was according to the definite plan and foreknowledge of God.
B. It was not God's first choice.
C. It caught God by surprise.

Jesus's death was God's plan all along, since before the foundation of the world (Revelation 13:8). Those who plotted against Jesus sinned, but their sin didn't derail God's plan. In fact, in His goodness, God bends all sin to serve His purposes and to benefit His kids.

★ 3. Do you find God's sovereignty comforting? Why or why not?

Later in this section, there's another, more subtle, illustration of God's sovereignty.

4. **Reread 2:36 and fill in the blanks below.**

Let all the house of Israel therefore know for certain that God has made him

_____ _____ _____ _____, this Jesus whom you crucified.

The title *Christ* (Greek for "Messiah") had special significance for Jewish believers. Their ancestors had been waiting for God's promised Messiah since the fall. And the title *Lord* (which means "Master") would come to have special significance to Gentile believers as a reference to both the role of God and the character of God. Even though the early believers had not yet preached the gospel to the Gentiles, Peter used both titles in his sermon. God's original plan of salvation was in motion, and Jesus was both Lord *and* Christ.

Review 2:37–41.

After hearing Peter's sermon, those gathered in Jerusalem were "cut to the heart" (2:37).

5. When has the gravity of your sin cut to your heart?

Then, they asked the apostles a sincere question: "*What do we do now?*" Peter, echoing John the Baptist and Jesus, called them to repentance.

Repentance is good news, because by turning 180 degrees from our sin (which is the definition of repentance), we turn directly toward our Savior.

In 2:38, Peter said to "be baptized every one of you in the name of Jesus Christ for [*eis*] the forgiveness of your sins." Our English translation of the Greek preposition *eis* can be confusing here. *Eis* is translated in other passages as *unto*, *in*, or *toward*—it suggests more of a relationship than a sequence of events. Baptism is a symbol of salvation, not a prerequisite for salvation. Peter reassured the new believers that with repentance comes the gift of the Holy Spirit.

6. At the beginning of the day, there had been 120 believers gathered. When Peter finished preaching, how many were baptized and added to their number?

In front of the southern temple steps were numerous mikvahs—sort of like big bathtubs—used for ritual purification. These new believers could immediately submit to baptism as an expression of their repentance.

Review 2:42–47.

7. Update your timeline (page 18) to record that in the year 29†, the church was established and began to grow.

So far, everything we've studied in Acts has set up the *establishment* of the church. From here on, Luke follows the *growth* of the church, region by region, beginning with Jerusalem. In 2:42–47, we see a thesis statement of sorts, summarizing what happened after the first believers repented, were baptized, and received the Holy Spirit. As 2:47 teaches, *the Lord Himself* grew His church, and the believers got the joy of devoting themselves to the work He was doing.

★ 8. Some of the work the early church devoted themselves to is listed below. Underline work you've participated in. Circle something you'd like to experience for the first time or again.

- All the believers were together in unity.
- They sold possessions to give to anyone who had need.
- Every day they continued to meet together.
- They broke bread in their homes, eating together with glad and sincere hearts.
- They praised God together.

★ 9. Look again at what you circled. How can you devote yourself to this work? List three practical first steps.

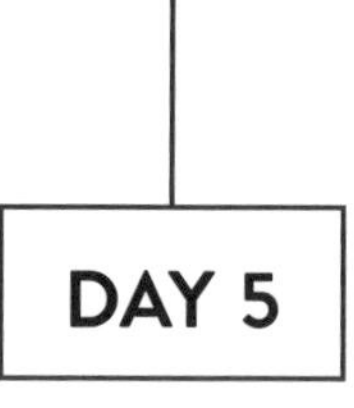

DAY 5

Acts 3

READ ACTS 3

Review 3:1–10.

Some time later, Peter and John went to the temple at the hour of prayer, as was their practice.

1. **Use a Bible dictionary to define the following terms.**

- Lame—
- Alms—

The lame man stationed himself at the most popular entrance to the temple at the exact time when many would be passing by on their way to prayer. And though his friends laid him at the gate daily, it's likely he had never entered the temple, not because of Mosaic law, but because of the religious leaders' interpretation of that law.

When Peter and John approached, he asked them for their charity. Little did he know that God had something so much better in store.

2. According to 3:4, what was the first thing Peter said to the man?

Can you imagine this scene? Because of Peter's instruction, it's safe to assume the man was looking down or away when he asked for alms. Perhaps shame or hopelessness kept him from looking at those on their way to the temple. But then Peter and John, filled with the Holy Spirit, looked at the man and he—at their instruction—looked back at them.

3. Fill in the blanks from 3:6–7 below.

> Peter said, "I have no silver and gold, but _____ _____ _____ _____ _____ _____ _____ _____. In the name of Jesus Christ of Nazareth, rise up and walk!" And he took him _____ _____ _____ _____ and raised him up, and immediately his feet and ankles were made strong.

In Judaism, the right hand signifies favor and blessing. The man asked for charity, but God showed him favor and blessed him with healing.

★ 4. When has our generous Father given you more than what you asked for? Write a prayer of thanksgiving.

The healed man could've done any number of things with his now-functioning legs. But his immediate response was to leap for joy and head for the temple, clinging to Peter and John, and praising God the whole time.

Review 3:11–24.

The man was healed for his good and God's glory. And because of the not-so-subtle scene he made on his way into the temple, there was a captive audience ready to hear the gospel. Astounded at the sight of the healed man, the crowd ran to Solomon's Portico, a covered walkway along the temple's eastern wall. And there, Peter preached another sermon.

You might be wondering, *Why were Peter and John at the temple at all? Didn't Jesus change all of that?* As we'll study together, early Jewish believers still adhered to many Jewish customs, traditions, and ways of worship, even as the early church grew to include Gentiles. Faith in Jesus wasn't a departure from their Judaism, but a continuation of it. Because of Jesus, they experienced the fullness of their faith.

Peter's audience at Solomon's Portico was made up of observant Jews and Jewish leaders who were at the temple for prayer time. Like in his first sermon, Peter began with a proclamation of Jesus's divinity and moved to a call for repentance.

5. In 3:14–15, what titles did Peter use to proclaim that Jesus was divine? **Use a commentary if you need help.**

6. Use 3:15 to make an outline of Peter's message to his Jewish audience.

- "and _____ _____ the Author of life,"
- "whom _____ _____ from the _____."
- "To this we are _____."

We'll see this message repeated a few times in Acts sermons: "*You killed Him, God raised Him, and we witnessed it.*" But Peter didn't leave them hopeless. He reminded them of the gift of faith.

Pointing to the reason they'd all gathered in Solomon's Portico in the first place, Peter told them the man was healed because of faith in Jesus. The power to heal didn't come from merely saying Jesus's name; the power to heal came from Jesus Himself.

Peter told the crowd that he knew they'd acted out of ignorance and that God's plan had been fulfilled. But he *didn't* tell them their actions weren't sin. Unintentional sin is still sin (Leviticus 4:2–3; Romans 3:23), and God forgives.

★ 7. Write the good news from 3:19 in your own words.

Review 3:25–26.

Through Abraham, God promised to bless all of humanity. Peter reminded the Jewish audience that Jesus was the one they'd been waiting for and that He had been sent to Abraham's descendants first. This new covenant would be a fulfillment of the old and would be opened to all who believe in Jesus. Praise Jesus! He made the way for us to be with the Father, and He's where the joy is!

8. What stood out to you most in this week's study? Why?

9. What did you learn or relearn about God and His character this week?

DAY 6

Corresponding Psalm & Prayer

READ PSALM 133

1. What correlation do you see between Psalm 133 and this week's study?

2. What portions of this psalm stand out to you most?

3. Close by praying this prayer aloud:

Father,

You are good, and You give every good gift! You didn't leave Your people without hope; You sent Your Son. And You didn't leave Your disciples without help after Jesus's ascension; You sent Your Spirit. Your plan since before the earth was formed was to send Your messengers to the ends of the earth to build Your church. We praise You that across generations, oceans, and continents, Your good news made its way to us, exactly as You knew it would.

We confess that we've made Your holy church a place of discord. Instead of seeking unity, we've sown seeds of division. Instead of faithfully preaching Your Word, we've preached our own agendas. And instead of worshiping You, we've worshiped ourselves. Forgive us, Lord.

Redeem Your church, Father. Remind us that we are Yours and that our Christian brothers and sisters are Yours too—even when we don't agree with them. Remind us that You gave us each other as a good gift. Lead us to true unity so that we may, like David, proclaim, "How good and pleasant this is!"

I surrender my life to You, Lord—every moment of my day, each decision I make, I yield my will and way to Your perfect will and way.

I love You too. Amen.

DAY 7

Rest, Catch Up, or Dig Deeper

WEEKLY CHALLENGE

On Day 4, you identified something the early church experienced that you'd like to experience today: unity, selling possessions to care for needs, meeting together daily, eating together in homes, or praising God together. You listed three practical steps you could take to devote yourself to this work. This week, begin taking the steps you wrote down.

WEEK 2

Acts 4–6

Approximate Year: AD 35

Scripture to Memorize

"As for the word that he sent to Israel, preaching good news of peace through Jesus Christ (he is Lord of all) . . ."

Acts 10:36

DAILY BIBLE READING

Day 1: Acts 4:1–22

Day 2: Acts 4:23–37

Day 3: Acts 5:1–16

Day 4: Acts 5:17–42

Day 5: Acts 6

Day 6: Psalm 118

Day 7: Catch-Up Day

Corresponds to Day 321 of *The Bible Recap*.

WEEKLY CHALLENGE

See page 67 for more information.

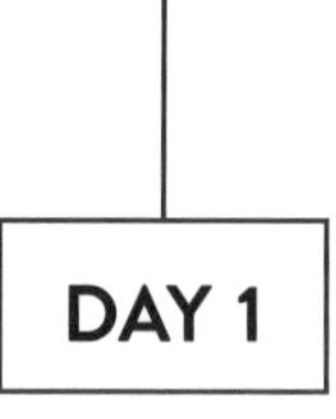

Acts 4:1–22

1. **Review 4:1–12.** Update your timeline (page 18) to record that in the year 35, persecution of Christians began.

At the end of Acts 3, Peter and John were boldly proclaiming the message of Christ, His power, and His role in God's plan of redemption. Acts 4 picks up midsermon, but instead of continuing their message, they were interrupted.

2. **Use a Bible dictionary or commentary to find out more about these people mentioned in 4:1.**

Priests	
Captain of the temple	
Sadducees	

Various groups and individuals opposed the message that was being proclaimed, and many among the opposition had political power. As Peter and John claimed Jesus had been raised from the dead, they were forcibly seized and held in prison overnight. Their claim flew in the face of the Sadducees' belief that there was no resurrection or afterlife. Despite the religious leaders' attempts to slow and silence the gospel message, the number of believers grew by thousands.

★ 3. Why do you think the number of believers grew instead of declined in the face of persecution?

After John and Peter spent a night in prison, the religious rulers gathered to determine their fate. The same powerful men who condemned Jesus to death asked about the authority of these two Galilean fishermen. It seems the rulers were saying, "*We put your leader to death. Don't you know what we're capable of?*"

4. **Look up the word *filled* (4:8) in a lexicon.** Was this type of filling by the Holy Spirit a temporary incident, or was it an ongoing filling? Why might that be important to distinguish?

The religious rulers attempted to flaunt their authority to intimidate the believers, but Peter's response made them look foolish! He quoted a Scripture they held as authoritative, using Psalm 118 to point to the deity of Jesus. Peter's response wasn't from his own understanding, but from the wisdom of the Holy Spirit.

Every builder in first-century Israel would've known how to build with stone because that was the primary material available in the desert.

Without a cornerstone, there is no foundation. Without Jesus, there is no salvation.

Review 4:13–22.

★ 5. What made it evident that Peter and John had been with Jesus, according to 4:13? Can this be said of your life? Why or why not?

While the gathered council didn't like what Peter said, they couldn't refute it. After sending Peter and John away, the religious leaders spoke candidly about their own bewilderment. Peter and John weren't educated men, but they had something far better than a formal education. They had spent three years in the inner circle of the Cornerstone of their salvation. They had learned from Him, and in His absence, they had received His promised Holy Spirit.

DAY 2

Acts 4:23–37

 **READ ACTS 4:23–37**

Review 4:23–31.

In the New Testament, believers often gathered to pray when one of them faced significant hardship. So when John and Peter were released, their first stop was to give an update to those who had been praying for them. The group's response to the news was a unified heart of worship.

Their prayer is a peek into the hearts of these early believers. They began by praising God for who He is and recognizing His grandeur in relation to themselves. This seems to have set their posture to see beyond their own lives and circumstances.

1. According to 4:25, who is quoted in the prayer of Psalm 2?

   A. David

   B. The Holy Spirit

   C. Both of the above

The early church understood Scripture to be God's inspired Word, so they knew David's words were actually God's words. The quoted passage from Psalm 2 displayed David's complete and total confidence that God would be victorious. The believers held the same view of their lives and chose to pray God's words back to Him—likely as a reminder for themselves.

Their prayer transitioned from David's circumstances to their own reality. Jesus was appointed by God, and His enemies could do only what was already in God's plan—no more, no less. Though the death of Jesus was horrendous, it made eternal life and salvation possible!

2. The boldness of Peter and John astonished the rulers and revealed that they had been with Jesus (4:13). In 4:29–30, the believers, facing threats, prayed only one request. What was it? Why do you think they prayed this? What would you have prayed for if you had been in their shoes?

These believers were convinced God was going to continue to work in power, and they desperately wanted to be a part of it. They had a keen awareness that any good they were able to accomplish was due to God at work *through* them. Viewing God and the work they were doing in this light allowed them to continue in strength without shouldering the weight themselves.

★ 3. Do you view serving God as something you have to do for Him or as something He does through you? Why is the distinction important?

Review 4:32–37.

Before you sell all your possessions and start a commune in the country, remember what we covered in the introduction about the difference between information and instruction. What we see here is a beautiful picture of the type of unity the early believers shared. There were several thousand believers in Jerusalem, and they were facing daily persecution and threats. Their survival required them to look out for one another and care for the needs of those in their immediate circles. And that way of life seems like it brought them a lot of joy!

★ 4. What are some ways the local church body supports and takes care of each other today?

This group of Christ-followers didn't have a consumer mentality; everyone had a part to play in building up the local body of believers. In place of selfishness was sacrifice; in place of pride was humility. The Lord provided power and grace in the midst of it all. The apostles were giving their testimony of the resurrection of Jesus, and they were put in charge of distributing resources to ensure all were cared for.

In the final verses of this chapter of Acts, we meet a man with a key supporting role throughout the rest of our study: Barnabas.

5. To get to know him, fill in the blanks in his profile below.

- Actual name:
- Nickname given by the apostles:
- Meaning of his nickname:
- Hebrew lineage:
- Native of:
- Sold his:
- Did this with his profit:

Acts 5:1–16

READ ACTS 5:1–16

Review 5:1–11.

Yesterday's study closed with Joseph/Barnabas—and lots of other people—selling their property and giving the money to the elders to distribute it as needed. In today's reading, Ananias took a page from their book but added his own crafty tweak. He performed the same type of "generous" activity, but without disclosing the truth to the apostles: He withheld some of the money. And because his wife Sapphira partnered in what he was doing, she bore the guilt of his sin as well. While they likely expected praise, they received rebuke.

1. According to 5:3–4, who was Ananias lying to? Who inspired this lie?

The great irony here is that God, who knows all, cannot be deceived. Although they were free to do whatever they wanted with the land—they could've kept the land, openly given only a portion, or even sold it and kept all the money—what they were *not* free to do was lie to God.

Their deceit broke trust with God's people, and God responded swiftly and righteously. And the people who heard about it had an appropriate response: fear. Some scholars believe this level of judgment—God striking them dead—was unique to the early believers, while others believe God's severe response indicates Ananias and Sapphira weren't true believers.

2. What do you think? Why? Can you think of other passages of Scripture that support your position?

It's important to note that Peter didn't sentence this couple to death; he simply confronted their lie. And God granted Peter a kind of supernatural insight that Sapphira would die as well. It's safe to assume this entire scenario grieved the apostles.

3. What do this couple's actions indicate about their view of God and His people?

★ 4. Think of a time when you demonstrated service or generosity in a performative way, out of a selfish motive. How did that feel? What was the result?

In these bodies of flesh, our motives will likely never be fully pure. *And yet here we still are*. God has shown us great mercy in sparing our lives—not giving us the same punishment Ananias and Sapphira both deserved and received. It's what we deserve too. But because Christ's perfection has been granted to us, we don't have to fear that God will strike us dead when we sin. Instead, He empowers us by His Spirit to do good works despite our fallen humanity. God's actions toward this couple should produce a holy fear in us, but they should also illuminate His great kindness toward us!

5. Look up *church* (5:11) in a Greek lexicon, then describe it in your own words.

This is the first instance of the word *church* in the book of Acts. Jesus had promised He would build His church, and here we see His promise is being fulfilled—not despite the couple's deception but through it. The story prompted a righteous fear in those who heard it, which served an important role in directing the early church toward integrity.

Review 5:12–16.

6. Who was performing the signs and wonders among the people?

Signs and wonders were regular occurrences in the early church. This was God's generous answer to the prayer they prayed in 4:29–30. The people held the apostles in high regard, but—perhaps because of what they'd witnessed with Ananias and Sapphira—they hesitated to fully engage.

This helped distill the church to a group of people who had counted the cost and found the gospel of Jesus irresistible nonetheless. Bolstered by the absence of lukewarm believers, multitudes of wholehearted men and women began to follow Christ.

Meanwhile, the locals continued to seek out the apostles' power, bringing the sick to be healed. Some even assumed Peter's shadow could heal! Scripture doesn't indicate whether their assumption was correct, but this detail reveals how highly esteemed the apostles were among newcomers to the faith. And for the first time since the advent of the church, the message began to spread beyond the walls of Jerusalem to the surrounding villages.

★ 7. **Read Matthew 16:18.** What did Jesus say would prevail? And what would be no threat to it? In what current scenarios does this truth encourage you?

As we see the early church established, led by the apostles, we'll continue to see threats arise—both internally and externally—but take heart: No sin committed by anyone inside *or* outside the church will keep God from fulfilling His promise!

Acts 5:17–42

Review 5:17–21a.

Though jealousy wasn't legal grounds for arrest, the high priest and Sadducees seemed to think it was reason enough. This time, though, the arrest wasn't just of Peter and John, but "the apostles." We don't know whether it was a few of them or all twelve, but their good works, growing popularity, and hope-filled message were a threat to the religious status quo. So off to another night in jail they went, providing yet another opportunity for God to display His power in their painful circumstance.

1. **Look up the word *angel* (5:19) in a lexicon and write down the definition.**

The angel's message would have seemed daunting if the apostles had been functioning in their own strength. They'd been arrested in the temple for proclaiming Christ, but the angel told them to leave prison supernaturally and go proclaim Christ back in the temple! The fear of man would have scattered them, but the power of their message and the indwelling of the Holy Spirit had them in the temple at daybreak, cracking open their scrolls.

Be careful not to read yourself into this passage and claim a promise that doesn't exist. This story is a *description* of what happened in this situation, not a promise or guarantee that followers of Jesus will always be rescued from hard things. There are times in Scripture when the believers don't get out of prison. In fact, every apostle died a martyr except John. But church history tells us he died in exile on the island of Patmos.

★ 2. Why is it vital to understand whether Scripture is describing an event or making a promise to all believers before we make an application to our own lives?

Review 5:21b–26.

This scene unfolds like a comic strip. The guys who thought they were in control didn't really know what was going on, and they were not just confused, but afraid. This council had already seen a heavily guarded Jesus vanish, but they'd paid off a group of guards to lie about it. Jesus's disappearance from the tomb led to all sorts of chaos for them, so they must've been nervous when the apostles went missing too! But surprise, surprise, the apostles were in the exact place where they had been arrested.

3. Why do you think the people might have stoned the officials if they had taken the apostles by force? What does this say about the motives of the officials?

Review 5:27–32.

The religious officials (who put Christ to death) may have been motivated by popular opinion, but the apostles doubled down on where their motivation stemmed from.

4. Using 5:27–32, fill in the table below.

What motivates the apostles	What doesn't motivate the apostles

Remember that this group of men were called apostles because they had been with Jesus. They had been there when He lived, died, and rose again. They weren't sticking to their guns out of a sense of moral conviction, but out of a dedication to the eternity-transforming truth they'd seen with their own eyes.

Review 5:33–42.

In his gospel, Luke recorded Jesus's harsh criticism of the Pharisees (Luke 11:37–44). He called them hypocrites, fools, neglectful, prideful, and more! It seems at least some of the Pharisees took these rebukes to heart.

5. Write down everything we know or can deduce about Gamaliel from this passage. **Use a commentary for assistance.**

6. What does this passage reveal about the schemes of man and the sovereign plan of God?

As a Pharisee, Gamaliel must have been a rare exception. While he apparently wasn't on board with this radical sect of Jews, he was wise enough to know that opposing God was a bad idea!

★ 7. What do you think the apostles might have looked like (physically) when they were released? Why do you think they rejoiced over their suffering?

No beating or berating would extinguish the apostles' passion. True to their word before the council, they preached openly—from the most public of venues to the most private—that Jesus was the long-awaited Savior. The message of the gospel would not be silenced.

DAY 5

Acts 6

READ ACTS 6

Review 6:1–7.

In the midst of persecution from both Rome and the unbelieving Jews, the leaders of the church made sure food was distributed to the believers in Jerusalem. But the church was growing rapidly, and growth often brings new problems. In this case, one particular group—the Hellenists—noticed that their widows weren't getting sufficient food. The Hellenists were Greek-speaking Jews who had moved away from the area and then returned. The fact that these "outsiders" felt safe to bring their complaint to the disciples reveals a lot about the culture of the early church—as does the disciples' response.

The apostles not only heard this valid complaint from the Hellenists, but took it seriously enough to gather *all* the disciples to discuss it and solve it.

1. What two things did the disciples need to focus on instead of personally serving the widows?

It's not that serving these widows was beneath the disciples; instead, the growing church required them to delegate tasks so order could be established and no needs would go unnoticed or unmet.

2. Circle the three characteristics that were required of those who would fill this new role.

They must be married.

They must be single.

They must have a good reputation.

They must be willing to serve.

They must be filled with the Holy Spirit (true believers).

They must be wise.

They must be patient.

The disciples weren't flippant about filling this role to serve the widows. The seven men selected—possibly one for each day of the week—needed to demonstrate respectable character and evidence of true salvation. (In the days of the early church, there was much concern that enemies might be posing as believers to mount an internal rebellion or otherwise sabotage them.)

3. Of the men listed, whose character is further highlighted? What does Scripture say about him?

The apostles prayed and laid their hands on them. Laying hands on someone was a common practice in both the Old and New Testaments—to bless, to heal, to commission for a specific role, and more (Numbers 8:10; Numbers 27:18; Matthew 19:13–15; Mark 5:23; Acts 13:3).

★ 4. Are you, or have you ever been, part of a church tradition that practices laying hands on people for prayer or commissioning? Briefly describe your view of this practice, and reference Scripture if possible.

Similar to other acts, like baptism, the laying on of hands is *at least* symbolic, but possibly serves to demonstrate the melding of the physical and spiritual realms. It's considered a means of grace. And while Scripture doesn't mandate it or establish rules around it, the Bible does reveal it as a practice the early church esteemed and took seriously.

In 6:7, Luke gives us the first of several summary updates throughout the book. And at this point, things in the early church were up and to the right in all the areas that mattered!

5. Match the phrases according to Luke's report.

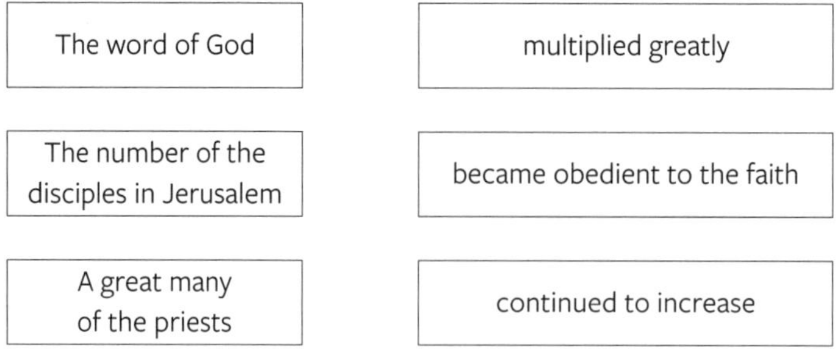

The word of God
The number of the disciples in Jerusalem
A great many of the priests
multiplied greatly
became obedient to the faith
continued to increase

6. Update your timeline (page 18) to note the first summary update on the growth of the church was recorded in 6:7.

Review 6:8–15.

One of those seven men was doing more than serving the widows. The Holy Spirit was empowering him to do signs and wonders among the people—not just among the church. This caught the attention of myriad enemies, who publicly brought charges against him. But the wisdom of the Spirit is stronger than any argument.

7. Fill in the charges brought against Stephen. Charges are combined in each section, so you'll need to separate them. (We'll come back to the final column in our next question.)

Verse	Charge	Similarities?
6:11 (part 1)		
6:11 (part 2)		
6:13–14 (part 1)		
6:13–14 (part 2)		

8. **Review the charges brought against Jesus in Matthew 26:59–63 and Mark 14:57–64.** For any charges that are similar to those against Stephen, put a checkmark in the final column.

Stephen's enemies incited men against him, set up false witnesses, and accused him of things he never said or did. Those who didn't believe Jesus was God would view it as blasphemy to say Jesus was greater than Moses and equal with God. Those who didn't believe in Jesus didn't understand that His words about the destruction of the temple (John 2:19–21) were His way of referring to His own death and resurrection. And they certainly didn't understand that He came to fulfill the law, not abolish it (Matthew 5:17).

As he faced these powerful men who wanted him dead, Stephen seemed to radiate a peace and joy that caught the attention even of his accusers. He demonstrated a humble confidence in the goodness and sovereignty of God. And this resilient peace wasn't just available to Stephen—it's available to all of us through the indwelling presence of the Holy Spirit. No matter what we face in life or death, He's where the joy is!

★ 9. In what circumstances do you most need to lean into the peace that comes from the Holy Spirit's presence?

10. What stood out to you most in this week's study? Why?

11. What did you learn or relearn about God and His character this week?

DAY 6

Corresponding Psalm & Prayer

READ PSALM 118

1. What correlation do you see between Psalm 118 and this week's study?

2. What portions of this psalm stand out to you most?

3. Close by praying this prayer aloud:

Father,

This is the day that You have made; let me rejoice and be glad in it. You are my strength, my song, and my salvation. Your steadfast love endures forever, and nothing can stop Your promises from coming true!

You are the cornerstone of Your church, but I confess that I've often made myself the cornerstone in my own life. I've been selfish and have refused to share what You generously gave me. Or I've been outwardly generous, with secret selfish motives. I've labeled minor inconveniences as suffering. And when I've actually suffered, I've used it as an excuse to stop seeking You.

It's tempting to ask for the endurance of Peter and John, or the peace of Stephen, or the strength of the psalmist. But they can't be credited for their endurance, peace, or strength. It was all Your doing. So I ask for the endurance, peace, and strength that only You can give. Remind me that You are on my side and that I have nothing to fear.

I surrender my life to You, Lord—every moment of my day, each decision I make, I yield my will and way to Your perfect will and way.

I love You too. Amen.

DAY 7

Rest, Catch Up, or Dig Deeper

WEEKLY CHALLENGE

On Day 1, we read that John and Peter were arrested for preaching boldly in the temple and then spoke boldly before the council. After they recounted their experience to their friends, the believers asked God for *more* boldness. They knew the only reason they had boldness in the moments they needed it was that the Holy Spirit granted it to them; if they were going to continue their work, they would need the Holy Spirit to continue granting it to them. Every day this week, pray for boldness to share the message of Christ and look for opportunities to be bold!

WEEK 3

Acts 7–9

Approximate Years: AD 35–36

Scripture to Memorize

". . . you yourselves know what happened throughout all Judea, beginning from Galilee after the baptism that John proclaimed: . . ."

Acts 10:37

DAILY BIBLE READING

Day 1: Acts 7

Day 2: Acts 8:1–25

Day 3: Acts 8:26–40

Day 4: Acts 9:1–19

Day 5: Acts 9:20–43

Day 6: Psalm 31

Day 7: Catch-Up Day

Corresponds to Days 322 and 323 of *The Bible Recap*.

WEEKLY CHALLENGE

See page 91 for more information.

DAY 1

Acts 7

Review 7:1–50.

The religious leaders had accused Stephen of blaspheming Moses, blaspheming God, and speaking against the temple and the law. At first glance, it may seem like he ignored these accusations. But Stephen didn't just give a history lesson. He cleverly emphasized key people, events, places, and actions of God in his account of Israel's history. God chose people through whom He would bring about His plan of salvation. God showed up in places outside of the promised land. But despite God's actions, His people were often disobedient and rebellious.

1. Write down the key people, places, events, and actions of God in the table below.

Verse(s)	Person or People	Place(s)	Event(s)	God's Action(s)
7:1–8				
7:9–16				

Verse(s)	Person or People	Place(s)	Event(s)	God's Action(s)
7:17–22				
7:23–29				
7:30–35				
7:36–43				
7:44–50				

Stephen's speech not only reviewed Israel's past, but it also pointed out a devastating theme throughout Israel's history. The people of Israel didn't respect or listen to the person God appointed over them.

★ 2. Next to the Scripture references below, write down what Stephen said about the person God chose and the response of the people.

7:9–10 (Joseph and the patriarchs):

7:25–28 (Moses and the Israelites in Egypt):

7:35–40 (Moses and the Israelites in the wilderness):

Review 7:51–53.

This was the climax of Stephen's speech. He made his main point loud and clear: Israel had always persecuted God's prophets, and his audience was no different! This group denied Jesus and was responsible for His death. They also denied the teaching and miraculous works of the disciples (remember their treatment of Peter and John in Acts 4). And they had clearly demonstrated their resistance to the Holy Spirit and total disregard for God's plans and purposes.

It can be easy to read through Israel's history and think, *Wake up Israel! Don't you see what God is doing?* But the reality is we sometimes don't see what God is doing in our own lives. Or we may see it, but stubbornly choose to ignore it. Some days we might find ourselves acting like the Israelites or Jewish leaders and missing what God is up to.

★ 3. Ask the Holy Spirit to reveal any areas where you're ignoring or resisting God. Ask God to help you obey Him and demonstrate faith in what He is doing in your life.

Review 7:54–60.

The Jewish leaders clearly didn't like what Stephen had to say, and their actions confirmed his main point. They followed in their fathers' footsteps and stoned Stephen. Notice how the glorious language used to describe Stephen, what he saw, and how he died is contrasted with the hideous descriptions of the people and their actions. Stephen was a man chosen by God and used by God in a powerful way. He died full of the Holy Spirit, and his last words requested forgiveness for his enemies.

4. Who watched the coats of those who stoned Stephen?

DAY 2

Acts 8:1–25

Review 8:1–3.

Not only did Saul keep track of everyone's coats, but he approved of Stephen's execution. Stephen's death had tremendous consequences for the newly formed church in Jerusalem.

1. What happened to the church, and who was the main instigator?

Throughout Acts, Luke uses summary statements or transitions to wrap up one section and alert us that the story is moving in a new direction. Luke made sure to include a brief mention of Stephen's burial and the lamentation for him; it was important for the believers to honor him regardless of the danger they faced. The persecution of the church sent believers out from Jerusalem and into Judea and Samaria. Despite Saul's evil attempts to eradicate these followers of Jesus, God's plan continued to prevail!

2. **Reread 1:8.** Shade in the bullseye below, noting where the believers have already witnessed and where they are headed to next.

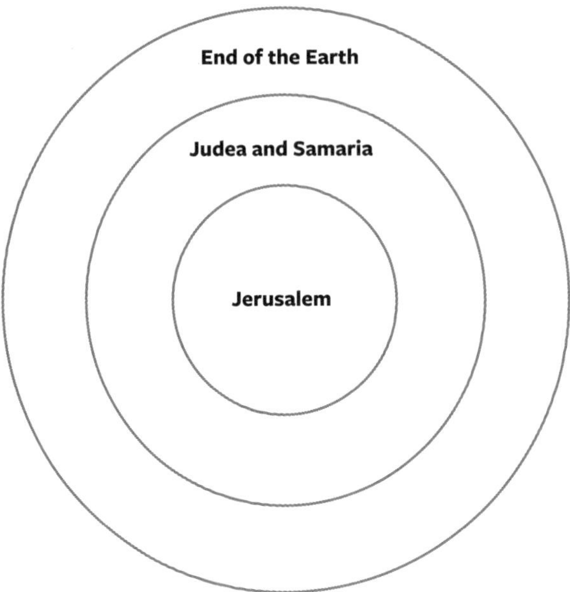

Review 8:4–8.

3. Update your timeline (page 18) to record that in the year 35, Philip went to Samaria.

Philip, who worked closely with Stephen in Acts 6, made quick use of the time in a new city and preached to the Samaritans. This was revolutionary! The Jews considered the Samaritans unclean because of their genetic heritage. Although they had the Torah—the first five books of the Bible—and claimed to worship Yahweh (just not in Jerusalem), Samaritans were hated by the Jews. Yet they welcomed Philip with open arms and open ears. Notice the radical difference between the response of the Samaritans and that of the Jewish leaders in Jerusalem.

★ 4. Why did the Samaritans listen to Philip? What was their response?

Philip preached boldly to the Samaritans. The message spread beyond Jerusalem, and the Jews confirmed that the believers took Jesus's teachings in Acts 1:8 seriously. The Holy Spirit also empowered them, as Jesus had said He would, to deliver the good news. Spoiler alert: This is only the first step toward "the end of the earth." There's much more to come!

Review 8:9–25.

5. Circle all the statements that apply to Simon.

- He had previously practiced magic.
- He was from Jerusalem.
- He amazed the people.
- He was humble.
- He said he was somebody great.
- Everyone paid attention to him.
- The people said he was the power of God that is called Great.
- He was Saul's cousin.
- He tried to buy the Holy Spirit's power.
- Peter rebuked him.
- He believed and was baptized.

As the good news spread to non-Jews, the disciples and believers often encountered other religious practices. Sometimes this came with spiritual opposition, but in this story it didn't. Despite what's said about Simon's pride and magical practices, he believed Philip and was baptized along with many others.

★ 6. According to 8:14, who came to check out the scene in Samaria? Why?

It's not that the apostles didn't trust Philip. His credentials in Acts 6 were impeccable. So why were Peter and John sent? Remember, this was all new to the believers. Even though Jesus had ministered to some non-Jews, that was not the norm. The Holy Spirit was moving the believers into uncharted territory. Most likely, Peter and John were sent to confirm the experience of the Samaritans. When the Samaritans received the Holy Spirit, no more validation was needed! The Samaritans were unquestionably part of the believing community.

7. What did Simon offer the apostles in exchange for the power of the Holy Spirit?

Peter had harsh words for Simon's audacious proposal. Though Simon seemed repentant, we don't know the true state of his heart. But that isn't the primary point of the text. The story reveals a more important detail: The Holy Spirit is a gift, and His power can't be manipulated or controlled by humans. And in His power, the Holy Spirit confirmed that these Samaritans were now God's children. Praise God!

DAY 3

Acts 8:26–40

READ ACTS 8:26–40

Review 8:26–28.

★ 1. Who told Philip to travel on the road from Jerusalem to Gaza? What do you think was the purpose of this trip?

Philip was on the move again. He was used by God in Jerusalem, he was used by God in the city of Samaria, and here God was moving him again. God sent Philip to travel on a road in a desert place. If Philip was confused or unsure why God commanded this, he didn't show it. Rather than questioning God's command, he simply rose and went.

2. Circle Jerusalem and Gaza on the map below.

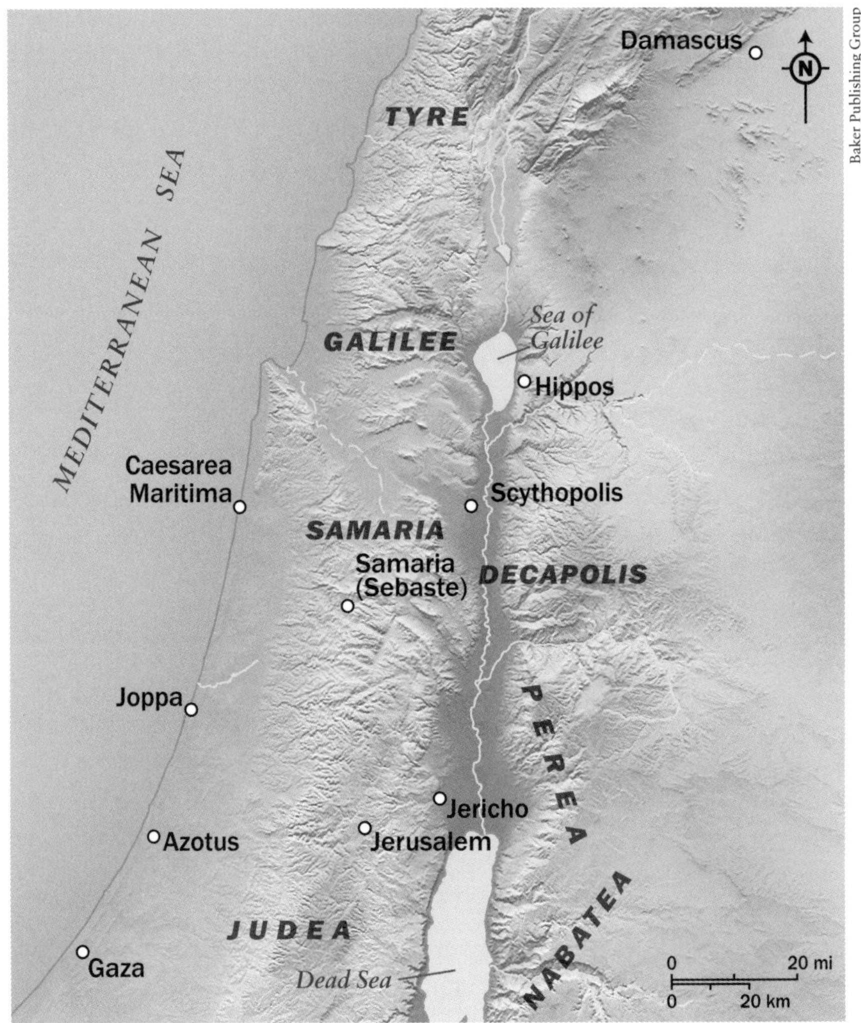

Gaza was about sixty miles from Jerusalem. We're not sure where Philip started out on this journey, but he quickly met the person God had prepared for this encounter: an Ethiopian eunuch. (If you're unsure what a eunuch is, use a Bible dictionary to find more information.)

3. Fill in the blanks from 8:27–28. Notice the amount of information Luke provided about this person.

And there was an __________, a __________, a court ______________ of Candace, queen of the Ethiopians, who was in ____________ of all her ____________. He had come to ____________ to ____________ and was returning, seated in his ____________, and he was ____________ the prophet ____________.

The Spirit told Philip to approach the chariot. This was the second time God specifically instructed Philip to do something. Clearly God had a plan for this situation. Although the Ethiopian eunuch had been in Jerusalem worshiping, the text doesn't reveal whether he was Jewish or a Jewish convert. What we do know is what he was reading: Isaiah.

Review 8:29–35.

4. What question did the eunuch ask Philip?

What were the chances that the eunuch would be reading this passage from Isaiah 53 as Philip approached his chariot? That chapter of Scripture so clearly points to the identity of the Messiah that many Jews are forbidden from reading it even today! Philip explained the text to him, helping him understand the good news.

Consider the different methods Philip used, through the power and prompting of the Holy Spirit, to share the gospel in Acts 8. He'd proclaimed Jesus to crowds in Samaria, where his message was accompanied by miracles and healings. And here, Philip patiently instructed one individual who had a simple question about what he read. The work of the Spirit in Acts reminds us that God used different ways to reach people with His plan of salvation. He used His disciples to meet people where they were. And He does the same thing today!

★ 5. What are some ways you've been prompted to share the gospel? Have you made assumptions about how, or to whom, the gospel must be presented? What can you learn from Philip's example?

Review 8:36–40.

In the midst of their conversation, they approached water and the eunuch asked, "What prevents me from being baptized?" The rhetorical nature of this question implied the response was *nothing*. We've seen this already in our study (2:38–41) and we'll see it again (10:47–48); once someone believes, the natural next step is to be baptized. Although there are a variety of views on baptism, we see in the Gospels and Acts that baptism was modeled after the Jewish ritual purification performed in mikvahs. Based on Luke's description, the eunuch most likely went all the way into the water with Philip by his side.

6. **Look up the term used for "carried [Philip] away" (8:39) in a Greek lexicon.** Write down what it means.

7. On the map at the beginning of this chapter, circle Azotus and Caesarea.

There are different opinions on what happened to Philip in 8:39. Some commentators are hesitant to assume a miraculous teleportation, while others claim Philip was in fact transported by the Spirit of the Lord to a new location. Either way, the primary point of the text is that he continued his evangelistic ministry and preached all the way to Caesarea.

★ 8. Based on your understanding of the Greek word and where Azotus is, what do you think happened and why?

Regardless of how exactly Philip left the scene, the Ethiopian eunuch went on his way rejoicing. Luke doesn't tell us what happened next in this man's life. Perhaps he went back to Ethiopia and shared the gospel with those in the Ethiopian court and palace. Or maybe God used him in a different way. One thing is certain: He was filled with joy. God had met him on a desert road, and he would never be the same!

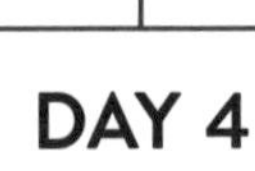

DAY 4

Acts 9:1–19

READ ACTS 9:1–19

Review 9:1–9.

Chapter 9 starts out with a stark shift in tone: "But Saul, still breathing threats . . ." Even though the gospel was preached to the Samaritans, Luke reminds us there was still a man adamant to stop this good news. Saul wanted to find and punish anyone associated with the Way—a name used to describe believers before they were called Christians.

1. **Reread 8:3 and 9:1.** Fill in the table below with Saul's actions.

Verse	Saul's actions
8:3	
9:1	

Damascus was about 130 miles from Jerusalem. This was not a quick day trip. Consumed by his mission, Saul was determined to go to any length to confront what he saw as a threat to Judaism. God, in His sovereignty, had other plans. He stopped Saul in his tracks on the road to Damascus.

★ 2. Write down what Saul saw, heard, touched, and tasted (include verse references).

Saw:

Heard:

Touched:

Tasted:

Jesus made two things clear to Saul in this encounter. First, He directly associated Himself with the people Saul was persecuting. What was done to a follower of the Way was done to Jesus. Second, He had another plan for Saul's life. And it started with a simple command: "Rise and enter the city." Saul obeyed and spent the next three days fasting—and waiting.

3. Update your timeline (page 18) to record that Saul's conversion happened in the year 36.

Review 9:10–16.

Luke doesn't tell us much about Ananias, just that he was a disciple. God gave him a special role to play in the unfolding story of the early church, and it all started with a vision from the Lord.

4. How did Ananias respond to the Lord in 9:10?

This phrase is used a handful of times in the Old Testament by people like Abraham, Jacob, Moses, Samuel, and Isaiah (Genesis 22:1, 31:11; Exodus 3:4; 1 Samuel 3:4–14; Isaiah 6:8). But Ananias's statement is the only occurrence in the New Testament. "Here I am" implied obedience and a heart ready for service to the Lord. This was significant because each person who answered the Lord's call had an important—and often difficult—task in front of them. Ananias was no different.

Notice the conversation between God and Ananias. God told Ananias to go to Saul and pray for him to regain his sight. Instead of immediately obeying, Ananias reminded God of Saul's reputation. Had God forgotten about the evil Saul had planned for the church or the letters giving him authority to bring believers to prison in Jerusalem? We know, and so did Ananias, that God had not forgotten all this. And His command remained the same the second time: Go.

5. What else did God tell Ananias about Saul in 9:15–16? Keep this in mind as Saul's story unfolds in Acts.

Review 9:17–19.

Ananias obeyed God and went to find Saul. When he spoke to him, he called him brother. Even before Saul said a word, Ananias accepted him as a fellow believer. God had told Ananias that Saul was chosen by Him, and Ananias treated Saul accordingly.

Just like on the road to Damascus, Saul's conversion experience involved his whole body. He *heard* Ananias's prayer. Something like scales fell off Saul's eyes and he regained his *sight*. He *felt* Ananias's touch as he laid hands on him. And he *ate* food and was strengthened.

Perhaps this is the first time you've ever read this story, or maybe Saul's experience is very familiar.

★ 6. Regardless, what stood out to you today in this incredible story?

DAY 5

Acts 9:20–43

READ ACTS 9:20–43

Review 9:20–22.

Saul had experienced a miraculous, life-changing encounter with Jesus. Even though he was a man steeped in the religion and traditions of Judaism he still needed time to consider the events that had just taken place. Saul had to reckon with reality: Jesus had altered everything he'd thought he knew. Saul was with the disciples in Damascus for "some days." These disciples likely helped Saul think through what it meant for him to belong to the Way. We saw Ananias come alongside Saul as a brother in 9:17; and here, Saul was surrounded by a whole community of believers. Throughout the book of Acts, we see that following Jesus is a group activity.

★ 1. Think about the different people God has used throughout your faith journey. List a few of them and note their significance in your story.

Luke masterfully captured the irony in Saul's story. In the beginning of this chapter Saul was "breathing threats" against the believers as he made his way from Jerusalem to Damascus. But once in Damascus, Saul spoke words very different from the ones he'd planned.

2. What did Saul proclaim about Jesus in the synagogue?

Well, that happened fast! Immediately after his study session with the disciples, Saul confounded the Jews in Damascus with his preaching. It makes sense that those who heard were both amazed and confused when we consider Saul's original goal.

Review 9:23–25.

Saul came to Damascus to persecute followers of Jesus. He'd come with letters from the high priest in Jerusalem. But Jesus changed everything, and Saul's life flipped upside down. Unfortunately, the Jews—most likely the Jewish religious leaders—weren't happy about this. Saul became the persecuted and was forced to flee the city to escape death.

Review 9:26–31.

Saul returned to Jerusalem as a fugitive fleeing persecution, and he wanted to join the believers in the city. But they were afraid.

3. Why were the believers afraid?

Remember what they had seen Saul do in Jerusalem? He'd approved the execution of Stephen—one of the pillars of their community. He'd gained legal grounds to drag them off to prison. He was one of the reasons many of their friends had fled to Judea and Samaria. How could they trust he had really changed?

Up to this point, God had used Ananias and the disciples in Damascus to help Saul. Here, God brought Barnabas, who assured the believers in Jerusalem that Saul's story was true. Despite being persecuted for his preaching in Damascus, Saul preached boldly in the synagogues in Jerusalem. Once again, opposition arose and Saul had to flee, this time to Tarsus.

★ 4. Fill in the blanks below to complete 9:31. What stands out to you in this summary verse?

So the church throughout all ________ and Galilee and __________ had peace and was being ______ ______. And walking in the _____ __ ___ _______ and in the ______ __ ___ _____ _____, it ___________.

5. Update your timeline (page 18) to note the second summary update on the growth of the church was recorded in 9:31.

Review 9:32–35.

The church experienced a respite from persecution, which previously had been a catalyst for growth, but it still multiplied.

6. Fill in the details from this story.

Who is mentioned and what is said about them?

Where did this take place?

What happened?

What did Peter say?

What was the people's response?

Review 9:36–43.

Peter was urged to come to Joppa, about ten miles away from Lydda. A widow named Tabitha (Dorcas in Greek) had died. Tabitha's death greatly impacted the other widows in the church. They showed Peter the clothes she had made for them; some scholars suggest these were likely the only garments they owned. This was a scene of great distress. But as we know, God has a habit of bringing peace and restoration to circumstances like this.

Peter knelt down, prayed, and told Tabitha to rise—and suddenly she was alive again! This story is reminiscent of when Jesus raised a widow's son (Luke 7:11–17) and brought Jairus's daughter back to life (Luke 8:49–56)—events Peter had witnessed. This miracle provided hope and joy for the widows who would once again be blessed by Tabitha's "good works and acts of charity." It also served to multiply the church.

Throughout Acts, we see great moves of God through the Holy Spirit. The good news will reach the end of the earth. We also see God's provision and care for His people in the church. God cares about reaching the lost *and* strengthening and encouraging the ones who have been found. He's where the joy is!

7. What stood out to you most in this week's study? Why?

8. What did you learn or relearn about God and His character this week?

DAY 6

Corresponding Psalm & Prayer

READ PSALM 31

1. What correlation do you see between Psalm 31 and this week's study?

2. What portions of this psalm stand out to you most?

3. Close by praying this prayer aloud:

Father,

You are my rock of refuge and my strong fortress. You see me. You hear me. You love me. You make Your face shine on me. Your goodness is abundant.

But I have treated the presence of Your Spirit as an item I can purchase or earn, instead of as a gift I was given. Remind me that You alone preserve the faithful. I have pointed my finger at Israel's wandering hearts, but I haven't examined my own. Reveal the stubbornness I hide from even myself. I have ignored Your prompting to share my faith and have cowered at the thought of rejection. Teach me that You give boldness and assurance, not fear.

Like Abraham, Moses, Isaiah, and Ananias prayed, so do I: Here I am, Lord. Make me strong and make my heart courageous. Lead me and guide me for Your name's sake.

I surrender my life to You, Lord—every moment of my day, each decision I make, I yield my will and way to Your perfect will and way.

I love You too. Amen.

DAY 7

Rest, Catch Up, or Dig Deeper

WEEKLY CHALLENGE

On Day 3, we read about Philip sharing the gospel in two different settings. Philip's story reveals the importance of meeting someone where they are in their faith journey. You might plant the first seed in someone's life, or you might be the one to see them believe in Christ. It's important to remember that God does the work of preparing hearts. Our job is to obey His call to share the good news. Below are some suggestions on how to do that. Ask God to direct you to the right option (even if it's not listed below).

A. Ask God to bring you a divine appointment like He did with Philip.
B. Ask God to bring a friend or relative to mind whom you can talk to about their spiritual journey.
C. Practice sharing the gospel with another Christian as preparation for sharing it with a nonbeliever.
D. Fill in your own answer here:

WEEK 4

Acts 10–12

Approximate Years: AD 40–46

Scripture to Memorize

"... how God anointed Jesus of Nazareth with the Holy Spirit and with power. He went about doing good and healing all who were oppressed by the devil, for God was with him."

Acts 10:38

DAILY BIBLE READING

Day 1: Acts 10:1–33
Day 2: Acts 10:34–48
Day 3: Acts 11:1–18
Day 4: Acts 11:19–30
Day 5: Acts 12
Day 6: Psalm 87
Day 7: Catch-Up Day

Corresponds to Days 323 and 324 of *The Bible Recap*.

WEEKLY CHALLENGE

See page 119 for more information.

Acts 10:1–33

A major turning point in Peter's life unfolded in Acts 10. He not only began questioning his tightly held traditions but also found himself standing before a door only God could have opened.

Review 10:1–8.

Here, we meet Cornelius and see a description of the type of man he was, both professionally and spiritually. Luke uses significant real estate to speak highly of Cornelius.

1. What do we know about Cornelius's spiritual practices?

Cornelius was a man who "feared God." While this meant he was respected by the Jews and even held similar traditions, there was still a unique distinction between Cornelius and the Jewish believers. A Gentile (non-Jew) who feared God was not considered a converted believer until he was circumcised. And even if he was a circumcised Gentile, he still couldn't associate with the Jews because of one simple thing: He was a Gentile. That is, until the revelation that happens in today's passage.

2. What specific instructions did Cornelius receive from an angel in 10:5?

Despite knowing little about Peter or the message he was to bring to them, Cornelius immediately obeyed and sent for Peter—a man he had never met.

Review 10:9–16.

While Peter was praying, God used something out of the ordinary to speak to him: a trance. This word may seem odd or confusing to us when we try to imagine what happened. But for Peter, God was using the moment to paint a clearer picture.

3. What command did the voice from heaven make each time Peter refused to eat what was unclean? What was the reason?

Peter was greatly concerned about this command from God—he even refused to obey.

The repetition alone tells us God was trying to drive home a point that Peter was not getting. He seemed to be more focused on his squeaky-clean record (literally) than seeing what God was trying to show him.

Review 10:17–29.

Meanwhile, there was a knock at the door, and three Gentile soldiers invited him to accompany them to the home of Cornelius, who was not only a Gentile, but a Roman centurion. For Peter, this would've felt wrong on so many levels. But one thing had become clear: The Spirit of God was the one guiding this interaction.

It's hard for us to grasp the magnitude of what took place here. That Peter even considered entering the home of a Gentile is shocking; this was unheard of in the Jewish faith.

But Peter, the visible leader of the church, represented the church's obedience to God's call in 1:8—to be His witnesses not only in Jerusalem, Judea, and Samaria, but also to "the end of the earth." For someone who held the letter of the law as tightly as he did, this wasn't just the end of the earth. This might have felt like the end of the world.

★ 4. Compare the emotions Peter might have felt as he made his way to Joppa with the emotions Cornelius felt when he welcomed Peter to his home.

5. What outburst of emotion did Cornelius show when Peter entered his home?

Perhaps the only thing that could've horrified Peter more than the thought of eating unclean food was the thought of being worshiped by man. His heart had been captured by Jesus. He knew there was no God but Him.

Notice the crucial distinction Peter realized in 10:28: His vision was not about food.

★ 6. What did Peter realize God had *actually* commanded him not to call common or unclean?

Do you see the application God brought him to? It's the same for us as well. Anyone who is in Christ is no longer unclean but washed entirely by the blood of Jesus. He is the judge of our eternal souls. Not us. It's common to judge others and hold prejudices like Peter did, or even to judge ourselves by our past sins and shortcomings. But if you are in Christ, you've been fully and forever cleansed. And what God has sanctified, let *no one* call unclean.

Review 10:30–33.

Cornelius eagerly gathered a crowd because he knew Peter had been commanded by God to bring him a word. He knew, beyond any doubt, beyond any prejudice, beyond any man-made tradition, that this was a holy setup—and that God had been listening to his prayers.

DAY 2

Acts 10:34–48

READ ACTS 10:34–48

We ended yesterday's study with a cliffhanger. Imagine the scene in Cornelius's living room: Peter gazed around the room of a Gentile's home, and numerous faces stared back at him in expectation. Despite all their cultural differences, they knew one thing to be true: God had sent Peter to them. As the crowd eagerly waited, Peter opened his mouth.

Review 10:34–36.

This proclamation, in the ears of Jews and Gentiles alike, requires us to stop and understand the weight of what Peter was saying. His first two sentences alone would've caused a collective jaw-drop.

1. Describe who God includes in His salvation. Notice the portion in parentheses and the weightiness this statement carried for Peter's audience.

While this news was good, it was not new. For anyone who had been paying attention, God had already told His followers that He was not a God of separation but of unity for all who called on His name.

2. Look up the Old Testament passages and fill in the table below.

Passage	Who was speaking?	What declaration was made?
Genesis 18:18		
Joshua 4:24		
Isaiah 19:25		

Review 10:37–43.

★ 3. Where did you see the gospel presented in this short discourse?

4. Where did you see the Great Commission (Matthew 28:18–20) presented?

Peter spoke of the prophets who foretold that this gospel would be for all peoples. But a higher Authority had also shown them by example.

5. **Look up the New Testament passages and fill in the table below.**

Passage	Who was speaking?	What declaration was made?
Luke 24:47		
Matthew 24:14		
Matthew 28:19		

★ 6. What does this reveal about the character and the consistency of God across the Old and New Testaments?

Review 10:44–48.

7. What event left the Jewish believers in the room "amazed"?

8. In what two ways did this manifest?

While speaking in other tongues (languages) is not always seen at the time of conversion in Scripture, this became a moment of holy confirmation for Peter and the other Jewish believers with him as they engaged with people who had a different native tongue. This small group of Jews and Gentiles gathered in Cornelius's home experienced their own version of what happened in Acts 2 when the Holy Spirit fell at Pentecost—where people of all languages were unified in their hearing of the Word.

9. In 10:47, Peter made a declaration that affirmed their unity in the Spirit. Fill in the blanks of this statement:

> "Can anyone withhold water for baptizing these people, who have received the Holy Spirit _____ ___ ___ _____?"

Despite all the questions that likely swirled in the heads of Peter and his Jewish companions during their trip to Joppa—and we can be sure their questions were many—one thing was certain: This was real. This nullified their tradition of tribalism and exclusion. God had used His Spirit to make it abundantly clear: He is not a God who divides; He is a God who unifies.

Then these new believers were baptized with water, just as they had been baptized with the Holy Spirit. This was a moment of obedience not only for the new believers, but for Peter as well. A clear acknowledgment that Jesus is Lord of *all*.

10. Update your timeline (page 18) to record that in the year 40, the first Gentiles were converted to Christianity.

DAY 3

Acts 11:1–18

 **READ ACTS 11:1–18**

As you read this portion of Luke's account, beware of the temptation to skim through the passage. Though this story will be familiar to you from Acts 10, remember that Luke, through the inspiration of the Holy Spirit, intentionally recorded it twice—though not without dropping a couple of new zingers to remember it by.

Review 11:1–3.

Instead of rejoicing in this report of God's Word reaching the Gentiles, the Jews couldn't get past Peter's seemingly reckless behavior of associating with uncircumcised Gentiles. This "circumcision party" Luke referred to would come to be known as the Judaizers—people who believed circumcision was required for salvation in Christ. The apostles and the Judaizers continued to clash over this issue throughout the New Testament.

★ 1. How did their man-made practices cloud their acceptance of God's purpose and plan?

Review 11:4–18.

While the brothers and sisters were focused on Peter eating with Gentiles, Peter started from the beginning and explained the events in order. The Holy Spirit's activity is laced through the beginning, middle, and end of this story, and it was all confirmed by the six brothers who accompanied Peter.

2. Fill in the table below to trace the Spirit's activity in this passage.

Verse	Describe the Spirit's activity
11:5	Peter sees a vision
11:7	A voice speaks from heaven
11:12	
11:13	
11:15	
11:16	

3. What did Peter, known to be a man of threes,* reveal about his encounter with the Spirit in 11:10?

Peter knew his audience. Standing before a group of law-abiding Jewish men and women, he could identify with their anger and confusion. If he had not experienced all this for himself, he likely would've had the same

* Some of the most important moments in Peter's life were accompanied by communications in sets of three. He denied Jesus three times (Luke 22:54–62), and three times Jesus asked Peter if he loved Him (John 21:15–19).

questions they did. As he recounted his experience, he explained how, at first, he dug his heels in against the Spirit's command.

4. **Reread 11:12.** How did Peter know he was supposed to go with the men who visited him?

When the Spirit spoke to Peter, he would've remembered Jesus's words in John 16:13, "When the Spirit of truth comes, he will guide you into all the truth"—a promise that still applies to us today.

5. Peter dropped zinger number one in 11:17a. Who was the catalyst for this event?

With that one line, Peter pointed out how God had leveled the playing field and broken down the dividing wall. God made no distinction. He gave the uncircumcised the same gift He had given the circumcised when they believed.

Zinger number two shows up in 11:17b. If Peter were holding a microphone, it would've been fitting for him to drop it and walk off stage. What more is there to say? He made the same point that Gamaliel, a Pharisee, made in 5:39: "If it is of God, you will not be able to overthrow them. You might even be found opposing God!"

★ 6. What does Peter's rhetorical question reveal to you about the power and sovereignty of God?

Whatever revelation you're having now, it was amplified for the first-century Jews.

In 11:18, we see a silent and dramatic pause. They had no idea what to say.

Despite his three protests at the beginning of these events, Peter had a complete role reversal; he became the one to convince the Jews of the Lord's work in the Gentiles' hearts. The Spirit lit a fire under Peter to lead the church in a new direction—and it worked.

7. What was their response upon hearing Peter's full account of the story?

8. According to 11:18, who was the initiator for the work in the Gentiles' lives? What two things were granted?

When God's power is the undercurrent of our actions, we need only obey His voice. The Gentiles repented and turned to eternal life in Jesus because God had granted them this gift. And the Jews couldn't argue with that.

DAY 4

Acts 11:19–30

READ ACTS 11:19–30

While some of the Jewish believers glorified God because of this door opened to the Gentiles, the excitement was not universal. As we've seen previously, persecution of followers of the Way had reached a fever pitch. However, in trying to extinguish this "sect" by driving out its members, the persecutors of the church failed to account for the power of the Holy Spirit. Their plan was foiled before it began.

Review 11:19–21.

1. **Look up the word *scattered* in a Greek lexicon.** To what does it compare this scattering of disciples?

Luke notes three places to which the disciples traveled. Note these on the following map, but put a star next to Antioch. This is Syrian Antioch, not to be confused with Pisidian Antioch, which we'll hear about soon. This Antioch, known for its sea trade and cultural diversity, became an important location for the disciples' ministry and future missionary journeys.

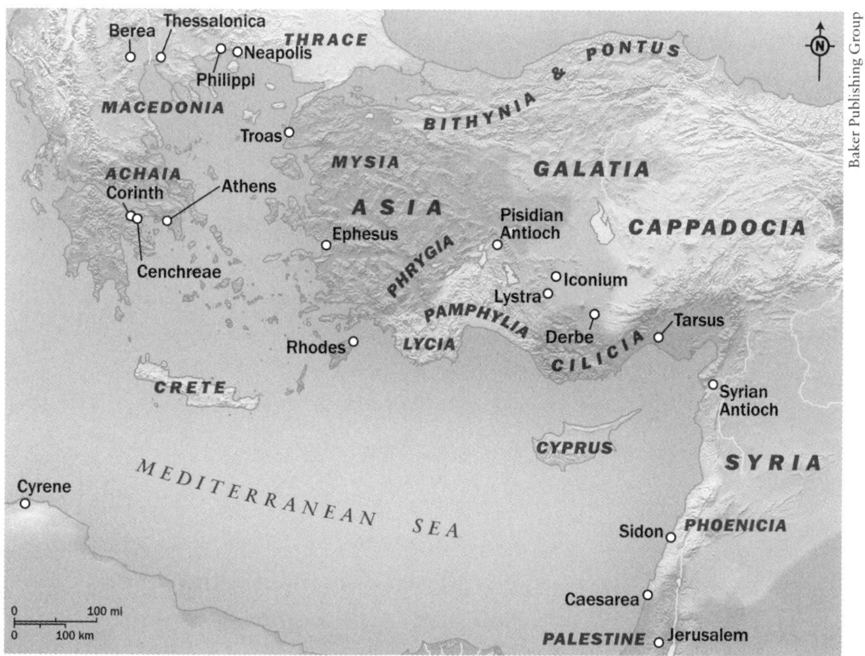

2. Who did the disciples preach to in Antioch?

★ 3. Why do you think some shared about Jesus only with other Jews?

The text doesn't tell us specifically, so we can only speculate, but it's possible the news about Peter and Cornelius had not yet reached these particular disciples. It's also possible that old habits die hard and they still had no desire to associate with Gentiles. What's important to note is that the gospel was still preached, and because of their faithfulness to share, the church was growing exponentially.

Review 11:22–24.

4. What was the exact count of believers added to their numbers at this time?

It seems the church was growing so fast, they stopped counting. By their best estimate, it was *a lot*.

5. What caused the church to grow at such a rate?

A. Persecution
B. The hand of the Lord
C. Both

While their tormentors were pushing them out of Jerusalem and Judea, the hand of God was on these men and women. In trying to rid the region of Jesus-followers, they actually sent light out into the darkness to impact more people for the kingdom!

Meanwhile, three hundred miles away, news reached Jerusalem about the growth happening in Antioch, so Barnabas was sent to see what was going on.

6. **Look up the meaning of Barnabas's name.** Why does this seem fitting for the impact he made on the believers there during this visit?

★ 7. How did he exhort the believers? In which of your current circumstances does this encourage you to be persistent and faithful?

Review 11:25–26.

Because of the growth of the church at this time, Barnabas realized they needed reinforcements. He knew Saul was the man for the job. Remember, Acts spans several decades. Even though we recently read about Saul in Acts 9, today's events took place approximately eight to ten years later.

8. What do you think Saul might have been doing during that time?

What we come to know about Saul later in his letters is that he was a disciple-making machine. Perhaps Barnabas, seeing the rapid addition of new believers, knew it was important that these men and women be trained in the Scriptures. After he found Saul and brought him to Antioch, the two men stayed there for an entire year, teaching this ever-growing population of believers. They became so notorious, the people of the region came up with a name for this group.

9. What were the disciples called? **Look up the meaning of this word in a Greek lexicon.**

Some scholars believe *Christian* meant "little Christ." While the term was perhaps intended to be derogatory, it clearly stuck and was later embraced. While the church's antagonists wanted believers to hang their heads in shame, what better honor could be granted to a forgiven sinner than to be dubbed "little Christ" or "follower of Christ"? Even as they suffered greater persecution, Christians would begin to "glorify God in that name" (1 Peter 4:16).

Review 11:27–30.

10. What was the disciples' response to this prophecy of a famine to come?

Despite all the struggles they encountered, this theme of unity and benevolence among the believers continues throughout Luke's account.

DAY 5

Acts 12

READ ACTS 12

Review 12:1–5.

When you see the name Herod in the New Testament, it can be a bit confusing because there are, in fact, several Herods in the history books. While it might be easier to ignore the question of who's who, we'd miss an important note about the state of the union. Herod the Great is the one you might know from the Christmas story, the one who tried to have Jesus killed (Matthew 2). Herod Antipas had John the Baptist executed and was on the throne during Jesus's trial. Herod Agrippa I is the one in today's story. Why does this matter? Because this particular Herod's prideful political agenda would throw gasoline on the Holy Spirit's fire—much to his chagrin.

1. List the acts of cruelty the church endured at the hands of Herod in just these opening verses.

James, the brother of John, was the first apostle martyred and the second follower of Jesus martyred. James's death was tragic; it reveals the political temperature of the day toward the church. But there's more to this story than meets the eye.

According to *Foxe's Book of Martyrs*, when James was sentenced to death, a man who had accused James was deeply moved by the apostle's countenance on the way to the place of execution. By the time they arrived, James's accuser, having observed the Spirit's power in his life, made a profession of faith in Christ! In the end, James's accuser had become his brother, and they were beheaded together for their belief in Jesus.[1]

2. Why did Herod have Peter put in jail?

Herod threw Peter in jail as a political move to keep peace among the Jews in the region and to beef up his own ego.

For the church, the situation was dire. Stephen was murdered. James was beheaded. Peter was in jail.

★ 3. How did the church respond?

The situation appeared hopeless. There was likely no one on the inside who could advocate for Peter's deliverance. So the church appealed to a higher court. Notice that their situation did not incite panic—it incited prayer.

Review 12:6–11.

4. Describe the level of security in Peter's prison.

It was humanly impossible for Peter to escape. Enter: an angel of the Lord.

5. What was Peter doing when the angel entered the scene?

The angel had to punch him to wake him up. What peace Peter must have had to be asleep in such dire, uncomfortable circumstances! The angel removed the chains, and Peter slipped away from the guards, past the sentries at the doors, and out the iron gates of the city. All of this took place on the very night Peter was to be brought before Herod.

Review 12:12–19.

You gotta love Rhoda, right? Imagine the scene as the church was gathered in Mary's home. This intercessory prayer meeting was seemingly devoted to one purpose—Peter's deliverance. When Rhoda answered the knock at the door, standing before her was the very answer to their prayers. So what did she do? She left Peter standing in the cold. Perhaps this was why the others didn't believe her report. Imagine them saying, *"If what you say is true, then where is he?"*

6. When they finally came to the door to see Peter standing before them, what did he instruct them to do?

You might be thinking, *Does Peter not know that James is dead?* But this was a different James. The James who was beheaded was the brother of John. Peter was referring to James the brother of Jesus, the now-presumed leader of the church in Jerusalem. This news would've been an immense encouragement to the persecuted church.

Upon hearing about Peter's escape, Herod had two choices before him.

7. Knowing his ego and his desire to please the Jews, which of the following was Herod more likely to do?

A. Acknowledge that an act of the one true God had taken place.

B. Accuse the soldiers of conspiracy and have them killed.

Herod's pride continued to lead him toward his own demise.

Review 12:20–25.

8. Why did an angel of the Lord strike Herod down?

Notice the order of events in Herod's death. Did you catch it? The text doesn't say that Herod died and was eaten by worms—he was eaten by worms *and then* he died. God will not be mocked.

In Acts 12, we face a difficult reality. In this chapter, one apostle is executed; another is rescued. Were the prayers for James less fervent? Did the church not muster enough faith for his rescue? Did God like Peter more than James?

★ 9. Has there been a time in your life when you faced similar questions?

For peace in the midst of sorrow and confusion, look back at 12:24.

10. Update your timeline (page 18) to note the third summary update on the growth of the church was recorded in 12:24.

We are not living in our story. We are living in *His* story. God showed that He was still moving. Evil had not won. His story would continue.

Bringing John Mark, the soon-to-be author of the gospel of Mark, along with them, Saul and Barnabas continued their work of spreading the gospel. No matter what these early Christians encountered, they could not stop speaking of what God was doing. They had found that even in suffering, He's where the joy is!

11. What stood out to you most in this week's study? Why?

12. What did you learn or relearn about God and His character this week?

DAY 6

Corresponding Psalm & Prayer

READ PSALM 87

1. What correlation do you see between Psalm 87 and this week's study?

2. What portions of this psalm stand out to you most?

3. Close by praying this prayer aloud:

Father,

You show no partiality. In every nation, anyone who fears You is acceptable to You. You've planned this since the beginning; You are the Creator of every nation, and from every nation, You call Your people. You've told Your people all along that You are Lord of all!

I admit I've put myself in Your righteous place, making myself the judge. I've declared others common and unclean. I've declared myself common and unclean. Forgive me, Lord, for believing and telling lies about Your image bearers, including Your children.

You turn orphans into Your children. You make enemies into brothers and sisters. You make strangers into family. Remind us that in You, we are united. Guide us in the way of unity. Teach us that unity—and indeed, every single one of our blessings—comes from You.

I surrender my life to You, Lord—every moment of my day, each decision I make, I yield my will and way to Your perfect will and way.

I love You too. Amen.

DAY 7

Rest, Catch Up, or Dig Deeper

In Acts 11, after overcoming the discomfort of stepping across the lines that divided Jews and Gentiles, Peter experienced the blessing that awaits when "brothers dwell in unity" (Psalm 133:1). Peter's joy overflowed to his fellow Jewish believers in Jerusalem. What had previously been a point of contention had now made the body of Christ even stronger!

Is there an area of division between you and another believer, perhaps even between other communities of believers? Is there someone in the body with whom you're missing out on the joy of unity simply because of your personal, cultural, or traditional differences? We're united with other believers eternally, but in some ways we allow our differences to divide us presently, missing the fullness of joy Jesus has for us. Seek to bridge the gaps in the body of Christ and build unity for the sake of the kingdom.

WEEK 5

Acts 13–15

Approximate Years: AD 47†–51

Scripture to Memorize

"And we are witnesses of all that he did both in the country of the Jews and in Jerusalem. They put him to death by hanging him on a tree . . ."

Acts 10:39

DAILY BIBLE READING

Day 1: Acts 13:1–12

Day 2: Acts 13:13–52

Day 3: Acts 14

Day 4: Acts 15:1–21

Day 5: Acts 15:22–41

Day 6: Psalm 16

Day 7: Catch-Up Day

Corresponds to Days 325 and 327 of *The Bible Recap.*

WEEKLY CHALLENGE

See page 143 for more information.

DAY 1

Acts 13:1–12

READ ACTS 13:1–12

Review 13:1–3.

Today's passage covers the first of Saul's three missionary journeys in the book of Acts. Luke sets the scene with five prophets and teachers worshiping in the church at Antioch. We're familiar with Saul's shady past by this point in our study. But he's not the only one with a past.

1. Who was Manaen a lifelong friend of according to 13:1?

This is the same Herod who presided over one of Jesus's crucifixion trials and beheaded John the Baptist (Mark 6:14–29). And some scholars believe the Simeon mentioned in this passage is the same Simeon who carried Jesus's cross (Luke 23:26). We see this dynamic repeated often in Acts: former enemies thrown together in ministry under the grace and mercy of Jesus Christ. Truly the gospel at work.

2. In 13:2, which of these does the Holy Spirit say regarding Barnabas and Saul?

A. "Set them apart for the work I'm about to call them to." (future tense)
B. "Set them apart for the work to which I am calling them." (present tense)
C. "Set them apart for the work to which I have called them." (past tense)

★ 3. Is there a calling you believe God has put on your life? If so, what is it?

Many scholars regard 13:3 as the first time believers were intentionally sent out by a church to another location to preach the gospel.

★ 4. In addition to praying, what were they doing in 13:3 before they sent off Paul and Barnabas? What had they been doing in 13:2 in addition to worshiping?

This is the first mention of corporate fasting in Acts, but we know Paul fasted individually in Acts 9:9. Throughout Scripture, we see a few reasons for fasting—repentance, grief, heart examination, and more. But here, they were fasting for preparation. Notice it wasn't done as an end in itself, because fasting is not just about abstaining from something—it's about connection *to* something. They fasted and worshiped. They fasted and prayed. Fasting was a means to connection with God.

Review 13:4–12.

5. On Journey Map One (page 15), plot each stop on the beginning of Saul and Barnabas's journey, referencing 13:4–6.

As they preached their way across Cyprus (Barnabas's home turf), they proclaimed the word of God in the synagogues first. Paul's missionary journeys took the gospel to the Jews first, then to the Gentiles. That process was God's plan from the beginning of Scripture, and we'll continue to see the ways that played out perfectly to spread the gospel to all nations.

The John mentioned in 13:5 is the same John Mark we met in 12:25. Note his presence, because he causes some drama down the road.

6. By what name is Saul also known, according to 13:9?

A common misconception is that Saul's name was changed to Paul upon his conversion in Acts 9. In actuality, as a citizen of both Israel and the Roman Empire, he probably would have been given both names at birth. Here is the first time Scripture mentions Saul (his Jewish name) also being known as Paul (his Roman/Gentile name). From this point on in Acts, he's referred to as Paul. However, this was not God giving him a new name, the way God did with Abram/Abraham and Jacob/Israel in Genesis.

Because Saul would be taking the gospel into Gentile nations, he used the Gentile version of his name (Paul). It's not unlike someone named John being called Juan when in Mexico. In fact, it's likely that in Paul's Jewish circles he continued to be called Saul.

7. Update your timeline (page 18) to record that in the year 47[†], Paul and Barnabas's first missionary journey began.

8. According to 13:11–12, what led to the proconsul's belief?

Just like Saul's experience on the road to Damascus, it was blindness that led to sight. Only this time, the blindness of Elymas led to spiritual sight for the proconsul. God used the very thing Satan intended to inhibit the gospel, Elymas's opposition, and worked it for good, to bring salvation to a Roman governor.

DAY 2

Acts 13:13–52

 **READ ACTS 13:13–52**

Today's passage continues Paul and Barnabas's first missionary journey.

Review 13:13–16a.

1. On Journey Map One (page 15), draw their boat journey from Paphos to Perga in Pamphylia.

2. In 13:13, what changed about our trio?

Bear that departure in mind, because it will play a key role in this missionary journey later. After Perga, Paul and Barnabas went on alone, north about 120 miles to Antioch in Pisidia. This is a different Antioch from the one we've been reading about so far, and it's in the mountains of modern-day Turkey. This region was generally known as Galatia, a name we might recognize from the letter Paul would eventually write to the churches of the region.

3. On Journey Map One, draw a line from Perga to Pisidian Antioch denoting Paul's and Barnabas's journey, and draw a line to the place John Mark returned to.

In Pisidian Antioch, Paul and Barnabas went to the synagogue on the Sabbath. A synagogue service of this time followed a standard order: opening prayers, a reading from the Law (the Pentateuch), then a reading from the Prophets. Afterward, if an educated person was in attendance, they were invited to speak. Enter: Paul.

Review 13:16b–33.

★ 4. Why might Paul have been inspired to lay so much scriptural groundwork in 13:16–33? **Look up 13:32–33 in the NIV to help guide your answer, if needed.**

A. To show off biblical knowledge
B. Because his audience wasn't familiar with the Scriptures
C. To fill time
D. To illustrate Jesus is the fulfillment of what God promised to their fathers

Up until 13:22, Paul's synagogue listeners would've recognized from Scripture and been in agreement with everything Paul said. They might've noticed how perfectly each passage flowed into the next, as if it were all part of the same story—which it was! But for these first-century Jews, the content of 13:23 would've been the lean-in moment. He told them Jesus was the promised Savior from the line of David.

★ 5. According to the standard order of the synagogue service mentioned above, what would have been read immediately prior to Paul being invited to say all this? In 13:27, what did Paul say they did not understand?

Review 13:34–52.

Paul went on to explain to them *exactly* how the words of the prophets were fulfilled. He listed one psalm and prophecy after another, revealing to them the ways in which the very words that had been on their tongues each Sabbath were the very words Jesus fulfilled in their lifetime. Then he offered them a sobering warning that was, in itself, a prophecy being fulfilled in their hearing in that very moment.

6. Use 13:40–41 to fill in the blanks in Paul's quote from the prophet Habakkuk, which he prefaced with "Beware, therefore, lest what is said in the Prophets should come about."

> "For I am doing a work in your days, a work ___ ___ ___ ___ ___, ___ ___ ___ ___ ___ ___ ___."

There's a common misconception about this verse. Scripture often speaks of joyful, wonderful acts of God that benefit His people. However, this particular verse in Habakkuk refers to a warning God gave His rebellious people: He was raising up the Chaldeans to destroy them. This verse would've served as a cold-water wake-up call, not a warm blanket.

Even though Paul preached a challenging message, the people begged him to return. But the following week, he didn't get such a gracious reception. Here, God revealed His sovereign timing and the plan He had all along. Paul and Barnabas spoke boldly, revealing that the Word was always meant to be spoken to the Jews first but they would now take that Word to the Gentiles. And it spread like wildfire.

7. On Journey Map One, shade the area to illustrate the gospel spreading through the whole region.

Shaking dust off one's feet was something Jews did when leaving a Gentile city, signifying that they would not be taking the essence of that city with them when they left. Here, Paul, a Jew himself, shook off the dust of persecution by the Jews, signifying that all he'd be taking with him was joy and the Holy Spirit.

DAY 3

Acts 14

Review 14:1–7.

Iconium was considered the capital city of Lycaonia, a large region north of the Taurus Mountains, in what is modern-day Turkey. As a result of Paul and Barnabas's persevering work in the synagogue, a great multitude in Iconium believed—among both Jews and Gentiles.

In 14:2–4, things got rough for Paul and Barnabas in this city, but they leaned in.

1. **Fill in the blanks below.**

"So they remained for a long time, speaking boldly for the Lord, who bore witness to the word of his grace, granting _____ and _______ ___ ___ _____ by ___ _____" (Acts 14:3).

"For ___ are ____ ___________, created in Christ Jesus to ___ ___ ______, which God _______ ___ ________ for ____ to do" (Ephesians 2:10 NIV).

God used Paul's and Barnabas's hands for the work, but we are *God's* handiwork. The work God did through Paul and Barnabas was work He'd planned in advance for that specific region and those exact people; Paul and Barnabas were simply the conduits. As are we, when we step into alignment with the mighty work of God.

Review 14:8–18.

After the attempt to stone them, Paul and Barnabas traveled to Lystra, another city in Lycaonia, where Paul was, once again, the conduit in a healing. Scripture says the man didn't just get up—he "sprang up"!

The locals were so awed by the miracle that they mistook Paul and Barnabas for Greek gods and quickly tried to honor them as such. Their speed may have been motivated by a local legend that the Greek gods Hermes and Zeus once visited Lystra disguised as mortals, and when no one except an older couple paid them honor, they destroyed everyone except that couple. At any rate, though the locals were quick to try to honor them as gods, Paul and Barnabas were even quicker to assure them they were just men—and only God is God.

2. According to 14:17, what earthly witnesses does God provide for all of humanity?

Many theologians refer to these earthly blessings as common grace—the good things here on earth that point to God's goodness and are available even to those who do not yet acknowledge the God who made them.

Review 14:19–23.

What a turnabout! First, the people of Lystra were desperately trying to treat Paul and Barnabas like gods. Then, a couple verses later, the same crowds were persuaded by Jews, who had followed Paul and Barnabas from their last preaching engagements at Pisidian Antioch and Iconium, to stone Paul.

3. What does 14:20 say happened when the disciples gathered about him? What do you think that means?

We don't know whether Paul was killed and raised to life again or just miraculously sustained during this stoning. Some theologians suspect the heavenly vision Paul described in 2 Corinthians 12 took place here.

In any case, when Paul rose up, he didn't give up and go home. He and Barnabas went to Derbe, then *returned* to Lystra, where he'd been stoned. The Holy Spirit had given him immense boldness.

4. After Paul strengthened and encouraged the believers in 14:22, what did he say?

A. God will never ask us to suffer
B. The Christian walk may include a bit of tribulation
C. Through many tribulations we must enter the kingdom of God

★ 5. Does this match your expectation of the Christian life? Explain.

★ 6. Based on what happened to Paul right before this, what might Paul have looked like physically? What impact do you think that might have made on his listeners?

It's tempting sometimes to believe the most impactful witness to others would be a life of blessing. Throughout the Gospels, however, we see suffering for the good news often served as a catalyst to others coming to faith.

Paul and Barnabas not only revisited these high-tension places, but remained there long enough to strengthen the churches so they could thrive in their absence and do so with wisdom and discernment. They appointed elders, and this is the first time we see mention of this practice in Acts. These elders were local leaders who could serve as shepherds in these local flocks. Note that just as when Paul and Barnabas were appointed and sent off at the beginning of their journey, these elders were appointed and committed here with both prayer and fasting.

Review 14:24–28.

At the end of their first missionary journey, Paul and Barnabas returned home to their sending church at Syrian Antioch.

7. What did they declare had been opened to the Gentiles? Draw this concept below.

DAY 4

Acts 15:1–21

READ ACTS 15:1–21

Today's study covers a unique event in the early church's history: the Jerusalem Council. It was a meeting of leaders in the church to determine what was required of Gentile converts to Christianity.

Review 15:1–5.

1. Update your timeline (page 18) to record that the Jerusalem Council happened in the year 50.

The council was initiated because of what happened in 15:1–2.

2. What did Luke say about the size of this disagreement over circumcision?

This was a big deal in the early church. The number of Gentile believers was growing like wildfire, and people were asking what should be done. It wasn't just the Jews who were disagreeing over it. The Gentiles wanted to know too: What was required of them?

Paul and Barnabas and some of the others from Syrian Antioch were appointed to go to Jerusalem to meet with the apostles and elders there. But even on this important mission, they couldn't resist spreading some joy along the way.

3. On the map below, plot their journey from Syrian Antioch through Phoenicia and Samaria to Jerusalem.

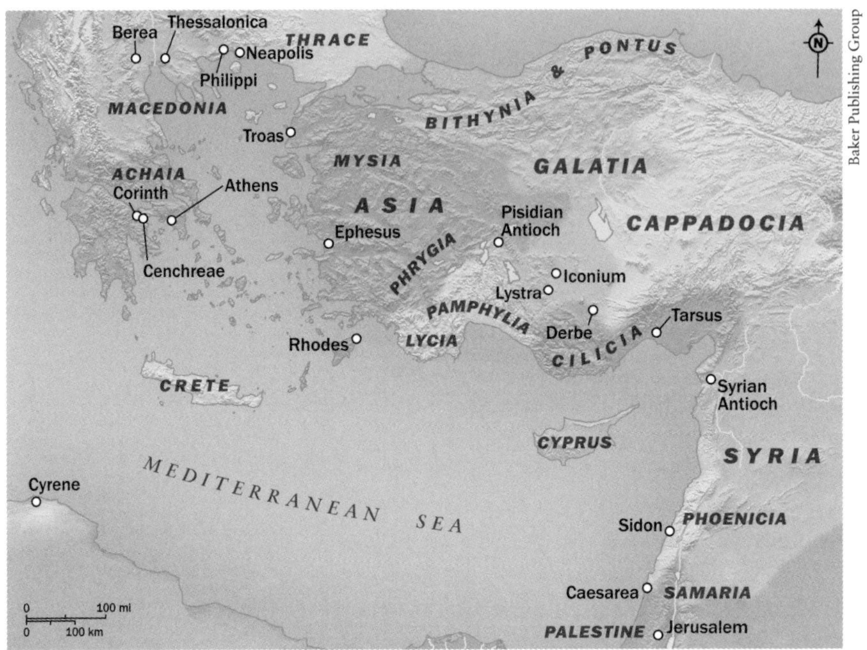

When Paul and Barnabas and their group arrived in Jerusalem, they were welcomed, but some Pharisees who were believers rose up to speak.

Notice that Luke mentioned *Pharisees who were believers* at this point in the story. When we read about the life of Christ, we primarily encounter the Pharisees as a hard-hearted group who opposed Jesus. But even in Jesus's time, the Pharisee Nicodemus inquired of Jesus to learn more about Him. And here at the council, though these Pharisees were apparently the first group to bring arguments, these were Pharisees who believed in rather than opposed Jesus. Those in attendance at this council genuinely desired to discern God's will.

Some earnestly thought the Gentile converts must first enter into Judaism through circumcision and live under the law of Moses before *then* entering into the Christian faith.

4. **Read Exodus 12:48–49.** What parts of this passage might the Pharisees have looked to as scriptural support for that claim?

For all their lives, they'd lived under the Mosaic law. Scripture was clear about certain requirements for foreigners coming into Judaism. So as we study this council today, bear in mind this was not a conversation between enemies or Jews in opposition to one another. These people wanted to discern God's will for unity on this issue.

Review 15:6–21.

Luke's account of the Jerusalem Council's meeting plays like a who's who of the early church. The speakers included Peter, Paul, Barnabas, Simeon, and James (the half brother of Jesus, not the disciple).

★ 5. Match each speaker to the evidence they brought before the council. Note that some speakers will have more than one piece of evidence to match with their name.

Speaker	Evidence
	According to Amos 9:11–12, God's plan was always to have Gentiles called by His Name—not Gentiles who become Jews.
Peter	God first visited the Gentiles to take out of them a people for His Name.
Barnabas and Paul	The signs and wonders God did through them among the Gentiles proved God was already working without their being circumcised.
Simeon	From the beginning of Israel's history, they've never been able to keep the law. Why would they burden the Gentiles with something they've personally been unable to bear?
James	Christian hearts are purified by faith, not works.
	God gave the Gentiles the Holy Spirit, just as He did to them. So if God has already acknowledged the Gentiles as full recipients of His work, why shouldn't they?

Based on these testimonies, James determined they shouldn't trouble the Christ-following Gentiles with circumcision.

6. In the list below, circle what James said they *should* abstain from.

- Things polluted by idols
- Sexual immorality
- Things that have been strangled
- Blood

Anyone who's ever eaten a chicken strangled on a farm (which is likely all of us who have eaten chicken) might be wondering what exactly they're referring to here. And this is where cultural knowledge is helpful in understanding why circumcision wasn't determined as necessary but these things were. Just because a Gentile Christian did not *have* to adopt the law of Moses did not mean that a Jewish Christian was required to *lay down* the law of Moses. So the four abstentions mentioned here relate to unity among all believers.

All four were related to ceremonial laws in Leviticus 17–18. The sexual immorality element didn't just apply to sex outside of marriage—it also prohibited marriage between most relatives. These marriages would have been a stumbling block to Jews, but they were culturally acceptable to most Gentiles. The other three related to dietary matters that would otherwise prevent Jewish and Gentile believers from sharing meals together. These abstentions weren't about adding any requirements to salvation—they were about bringing believers together in unity.

★ 7. Have you ever chosen to abstain from something to bring unity with a fellow believer? Or has anyone ever done that on your behalf? If so, describe the experience.

DAY 5

Acts 15:22–41

 **READ ACTS 15:22–41**

Review 15:22–35.

Today's passage picks up with the results of the Jerusalem Council's decision. They wrote a letter explaining their findings and sent chosen men to accompany that letter.

1. Who was sent in addition to Paul and Barnabas?

This may seem like a small detail at first. But note their mention, because in today's passage, we'll see another example of God's incredible sovereignty in the details—the way He provides and plans in advance *for* His people and *with* His people.

The letter explained their decision to lay "no greater burden" than four specific requirements.

2. What were they? And what was the heart behind choosing these four? (Refer to the end of yesterday's study, if needed.)

The four men took the four requirements to Syrian Antioch first.

3. What was the response of the church in Antioch?

★ 4. True or false: As soon as they had read the letter, Paul, Barnabas, Judas, and Silas immediately left for the next location. Explain your answer.

Review 15:36–41.

Here, we see a model of the early church growing in width *and* depth. Throughout Acts, Luke describes staggering numbers of people coming to faith. And the church continued to grow as the gospel spread from those regions, fulfilling Jesus's words in 1:8: "You will be my witnesses in Jerusalem and in all Judea and Samaria, and to the end of the earth." And yet, amid all this numerical and geographical growth, Paul basically said to Barnabas, *"Let's go back to every city we've already been to and check in on everybody."*

Though God's multiplication of the number of believers in this time was miraculous and stunning, Paul was not just about seeing how many people could come to faith. There was a clear emphasis on investing in these communities where the seed of faith had been planted, to teach and encourage the new believers to become strong and faithful people of depth, to tend that growth.

5. Who did Barnabas want to take with them? Why did Paul object?

We don't know the reason why this colaborer bailed back in Pamphylia. Perhaps Paul felt they shouldn't take someone who'd already shown he wouldn't stick around when the going got tough. We do know it was the cause of a huge disagreement that led to the dynamic duo of Paul and Barnabas going their separate ways. But wait to see what God does.

6. On Journey Map Two (page 16), plot the separate journeys of Paul and Barnabas in 15:39–41.

7. Update your timeline (page 18) to record that in the year 51, Paul's and Barnabas's second missionary journeys began.

What had been one dynamic duo became two! God sent Barnabas and John Mark back to Cyprus, while Paul took Silas through Syria and Cilicia. So before we're devastated by the band breaking up, let's note what just happened here. God used the ugliness of human discord to fulfill His purposes and bring good—and even better—from it. It's likely Paul and Barnabas bore in their hearts the weight of that relational fracture. Nevertheless, God gave each of them a new partner and fresh fellowship—and doubled the places where the gospel was being sown and tended. Praise God we have a Father like that.

Satan loves to use things like fighting and discord to make us feel disqualified, to make us think our relationships are so damaged we could never be useful to the Lord. But God does not call the sinless; He calls those He will sanctify.

★ 8. Write a prayer over your relationships that God would strengthen, restore, and repurpose what Satan intended for evil for God's better purposes and plans. Then watch to see what God does with it.

Remember that the early church was about both width and depth. God was making a people for Himself from all nations to sit at the same table and remain at that metaphorical table together as they grew in faith.

Today's letter from the Jerusalem Council was all about unity: How could these people groups from different cultures sit together at the same meal with Jesus Christ at the head? The unity among these believers was countercultural and unprecedented. And that is the gospel of Jesus Christ. He's where the unity is. He's where the restoration is. And He's where the joy is!

9. What stood out to you most in this week's study? Why?

10. What did you learn or relearn about God and His character this week?

DAY 6

Corresponding Psalm & Prayer

 **READ PSALM 16**

1. What correlation do you see between Psalm 16 and this week's study?

2. What portions of this psalm stand out to you most?

3. Close by praying this prayer aloud:

Father,

You created life and You give life to the fullest. You sent Jesus to fulfill the promises You made to His earthly ancestors, and when You send Him again, He will fulfill the promises You've made to all

Your kids. Because of Your great love, we are sure and steady when we join with David and say, "I have no good apart from You."

Yet I confess that I look to other places for good. I've fixed my eyes on the temporal, not the eternal. I've focused on what I don't have, rather than on what You've given me. I've obsessed about the things of the world, not on the things of Your kingdom.

Help me remember that only in Your presence is the fullness of joy. Reveal the calling You have for my life for advancing Your kingdom. Remind me that because of Your calling, even in the face of trials, I can say, "The lines have fallen for me in pleasant places." Show me that I truly have a beautiful inheritance.

Lead me. Counsel me. Instruct me. I surrender my life to You, Lord—every moment of my day, each decision I make, I yield my will and way to Your perfect will and way.

I love You too. Amen.

DAY 7

Rest, Catch Up, or Dig Deeper

WEEKLY CHALLENGE

This week's study covers a couple of moments when members of the early church fasted in conjunction with another spiritual practice—like worship or prayer. In these passages, fasting was done in a time of preparation, commissioning, or sending someone off for a purpose. In Scripture, fasting always pertained to abstaining from food. Carve out a period of time this week to fast and commit time to prayer. (If you have hesitations or limitations surrounding this, talk with your doctor and your pastor or mentor about how to approach fasting with wisdom.)

WEEK 6

Acts 16–17

Approximate Years: AD 52–53

Scripture to Memorize

"... but God raised him on the third day and made him to appear, not to all the people but to us who had been chosen by God as witnesses, who ate and drank with him after he rose from the dead."

Acts 10:40–41

DAILY BIBLE READING

Day 1: Acts 16:1–10
Day 2: Acts 16:11–24
Day 3: Acts 16:25–40
Day 4: Acts 17:1–15
Day 5: Acts 17:16–34
Day 6: Psalm 115
Day 7: Catch-Up Day

Corresponds to Days 327 and 330 of *The Bible Recap*.

WEEKLY CHALLENGE

See page 168 for more information.

Acts 16:1–10

READ ACTS 16:1–10

Review 16:1–5.

The people in Derbe had perhaps the best response to the gospel during Paul's first missionary journey, so this stop on his second missionary journey must've been an encouraging one. Some commentators suggest about five years had passed between trips. Though the text doesn't tell us whether Paul knew Timothy from his first visit, word of Timothy had certainly reached Paul.

1. **Using a Bible commentary, write a bio for Timothy below.**

It must have been an honor to be chosen to learn and minister under Paul. But the price of admission wasn't cheap.

2. Given what we know about the Jerusalem Council, why would Paul take Timothy to be circumcised? **(Use a Bible commentary if needed.)**

It seems completely backward for Paul to ask Timothy to be circumcised. After all, a large part of his journey was to tell the believers about the decisions that were made at the Jerusalem Council. Though the Council had decided circumcision wasn't mandatory, Paul was willing to go to great lengths to remove any stumbling blocks that might've prevented anyone from coming to faith in Christ.

3. Fill in the blanks below to complete 16:5.

So the churches were __________ in the ______, and they ________ in numbers _____.

4. What do you think the correlation is between strengthening in faith and increasing in numbers?

5. Update your timeline (page 18) to note the fourth summary update on the growth of the church was recorded in 16:5.

God wasn't just growing His church in numbers, but also in depth. It appears that numbers didn't increase if depth didn't increase, and depth consistently produced higher numbers. There was no rapid church-growth strategy or social media campaign, just intentional and humble discipleship.

★ 6. Do you correlate your spiritual growth with the salvation and discipleship of people around you? Why or why not?

Review 16:6–10.

Acts 16:6–7 might feel jarring to you. *Why wouldn't God want Paul to go to those people? Didn't He want them to be saved?* It's a valid question! So let's look a little deeper.

God desires that all might know Him (1 Timothy 2:3–4), and His perfect timing and unfolding revelation are also in play. So the *no* here is more of a *not yet*. We'll see throughout the New Testament that Paul does eventually visit almost all of these places. God uses both open doors and closed doors to guide His kids. In this instance, Paul was being guided by God via a closed door.

★ 7. Have you ever felt discouraged by God saying no to a desire of yours, only to later discover the better plan He'd been working out? If so, describe your experience.

Sometimes it's hard to see God's sovereign hand working all things for our good and for His glory (see Romans 8:28–30). This section seems to be as much about where Paul didn't get to go as it is about where he was called to go. Paul's eyes were on the region, while God's were on an entirely different continent!

8. Which of the following are true of Paul's Macedonian call? Circle all that apply.

A. He was already on his way to Macedonia.
B. He received a vision at night.
C. He questioned the call because he wanted to go to Asia.
D. They sought to go to Macedonia immediately.
E. He was sure God had called them to Macedonia.

There was a shift between 16:8 and 16:10 so subtle you might have missed it. Take a look and see if you can find it. Our author, Luke, went from telling the story about the journey to joining the journey. Luke was a member of Paul's traveling party. At this point, we know Paul's companions included at least Silas, Timothy, and now Luke. Can you imagine being a fly on the wall in that boat?

DAY 2

Acts 16:11–24

READ ACTS 16:11–24

Review 16:11–15.

1. On Journey Map Two (page 16), draw the route from today's reading.

Acts 16:11–12 gives us important contextual information. The people we meet in today's study will pop up again elsewhere in the New Testament; Paul used this visit to establish a church in Philippi, so be on the lookout for the men and women who would receive a letter from Paul that we know as the book of Philippians. Some notable people are Lydia, the demonized girl, and the entire family of Paul's jailer. By taking the gospel to these cities in Europe, Paul and his companions were acting in obedience to the Lord's calling. Their stops were considered "the end of the earth" even though they were technically still part of the Roman Empire.

While Jewish believers were no longer bound by the law, Paul still chose to observe the Sabbath. When Paul arrived in a new city, he always looked to minister to the Jews first; his time in Philippi was no different. The Jews here weren't gathered in a synagogue—perhaps there wasn't one—but by the river. This prayer gathering of women leads scholars to presume there were very few Jewish men in Philippi. If there had been an abundance of Jewish men, there likely would have been a synagogue for them to worship in.

2. **Using a Bible commentary, write a brief bio of Lydia, the first European convert.**

By including Lydia's conversion in his account, Luke continues to demonstrate that God sees and values women. Not only is she valued, but she is led by the Lord!

★ 3. The Lord opened Lydia's heart to pay attention to Paul. What does this imply about God's role in salvation? Does this challenge your way of thinking? Why or why not?

Lydia's baptism is our evidence that she decided to become a follower of Jesus that day. Immediately following her conversion, Lydia not only showed hospitality and generosity to these new brothers in Christ, but also exhibited a hunger and urgency for the truth.

Review 16:16–18.

4. **Look up the word *divination* (16:16) in a Greek lexicon and record its meaning.**

We know a number of things about this girl immediately: She had a spirit of divination, she was owned and exploited for money, and she was somehow able to tell the future. While it might be natural to assume a demon-possessed girl would be spouting lies, what she proclaimed about Paul and his companions was true. And she didn't just do this once; she was persistent.

5. Why do you think Paul might have been annoyed at her behavior and proclamations? **Use a Bible commentary for help.**

When Paul commanded the demon to come out of the girl, he didn't attempt to do so by his own strength, but by the power and authority of Jesus. It's important to note here that he wasn't claiming the power was in the word *Jesus*, but in the *person* of Jesus. In the ancient world, a name was not just what someone was called—it was a picture of their identity. Jesus was and is the Savior!

★ 6. What is the difference between looking for power in the word *Jesus* and looking for power in the person of Jesus?

Review 16:19–24.

It's clear that the owners of this formerly demon-possessed girl were more concerned with their financial gain from her fortune-telling abilities than with her as a person. We learn nothing about the girl after the demon was cast out. We can only hope that her freedom from demon possession also led to freedom from her spiritually abusive situation and freedom in Christ.

Her owners were upset about a lost opportunity for financial gain; their hope for security was literally in evil. In their anger, they seized only Paul and Silas to be presented in public before the local rulers. We saw before that there probably weren't many Jewish men in the city, and anyone who wasn't a Roman citizen was considered an outsider and therefore less-than. Timothy was only half Jewish and Luke was Greek, which is likely why they aren't mentioned in the arrest. The accusation in 16:20 comes across like they spit out the word *Jews*. *"After all,"* they seemed to say, *"as Romans, we're above this type of rowdy, illegal behavior."*

7. How would you describe the scene in 16:22–24 to a friend? **Refer to a Bible commentary to get a fuller picture.**

The punishment certainly doesn't seem to fit the "crime," but it paints a picture of the persecution faced by early believers so that we might have the gospel today. And as always, God had a very specific plan for this particular imprisonment.

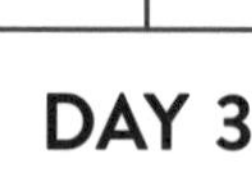

DAY 3

Acts 16:25–40

READ ACTS 16:25–40

Review 16:25–34.

Paul and Silas had been wrongly profiled, beaten, arrested, secured in leg shackles, and thrown into a maximum-security prison. Even in these treacherous and unfair realities, they were filled with joy! With prayer and singing, they reminded themselves of what was true despite their circumstances. Had they been focused on what was happening *to* them, they may have missed an opportunity for what God wanted to do *through* them.

1. Compare and contrast the prison stories in the table below.

Differences		
12:6–11	12:18–19	16:25–29
Similarities		

We see in these passages that the Holy Spirit didn't submit to a predictable playbook, so to expect Him to act the same in every circumstance misunderstands the sovereignty and goodness of God in every detail of our lives.

Greece is one of the most seismically active countries in Europe, so earthquakes would not have been an unusual experience, but this earthquake seems to have been different.

2. Circle all the descriptors that apply to this earthquake.

A. It was big.
B. The foundation of the prison was shaken.
C. All the doors were sealed shut.
D. Everyone's restraints were loosened.
E. All the rats attacked the jailer.

This earthquake was certainly a supernatural event, but it wasn't about freeing Paul and Silas from prison; it was about the salvation of the jailer and his household. If Paul and Silas had been focused on their circumstances, they would have missed the discernment from the Holy Spirit compelling them to sit tight despite the open prison doors.

In the Roman Empire, those guarding prisoners were to guard them with their lives. That meant if prisoners escaped, the jailers were subject to death. It may sound brutal, but it was probably an efficient deterrent for corruption. So when this jailer awoke and found all the doors open, he knew his life was over—one way or another. Until he heard a voice coming through the dark prison.

3. What was the jailer's response? What do you think caused him to recognize that Paul and Silas knew the key to salvation?

Amazingly, the jailer took Paul and Silas out of prison. The answer to his heart's question was brief: "Believe in the Lord Jesus, and you will be saved." This is an example of salvation by grace alone, received by faith alone. Some suggest that this is too simple, or they critique that this statement didn't include repentance. But the man had already demonstrated repentance with his response and was ready to believe.

The jailer took these two prisoners to his own home, where his entire household heard their gospel presentation. This man, who may have participated in the public beating, cleaned their wounds and was then baptized. Talk about a one-eighty! And remember the joy-despite-adversity Paul and Silas had in prison? It's turned into a salvation house party complete with food and celebration. They'd come a long way from having their feet in stocks in maximum security!

★ 4. Paul and Silas's posture of prayer and worship helped them discern what was required of them in their circumstances. In difficult situations, do you have a posture to receive discernment from the Holy Spirit? Explain.

Review 16:35–40.

Paul and Silas had left the prison in the custody of the jailer, had an incredible night of celebration, then did something astounding: They went back to prison *willingly*. Had they not gone back, the jailer would've still been on the hook for their escape. They weren't concerned about themselves; they recognized that this imprisonment was about him.

In the morning, cooler heads prevailed, and it seems the magistrates realized they had no legal grounds to keep these men in prison. They sent police to the jail to quietly have Paul and Silas released.

The jailer was pleased to pass along the news that his new brothers in Christ were to be released, but Paul hit the brakes. As a Roman citizen, Paul subjected himself to the law of the land. He was a good citizen, and he expected to be treated with the rights that came along with his citizenship. Paul wanted the justice that was due him. And once word got back to the magistrates that these Jewish men were also Roman citizens, they quickly played politics and swept the whole thing under the rug. Paul and

Silas received an in-person apology, an escort from prison, and a plea for them to leave. You'd better believe these magistrates would think twice before allowing a Christian to be treated poorly in their city!

Paul gave us an exceptional example of how to hold confidence and humility at the same time. He leveraged his Roman citizenship for the glory of the Lord and advancement of the gospel.

★ 5. Do you leverage all you've got to the glory of the Lord and the advancement of the gospel? Or do you find yourself separating your faith from other aspects of your life?

Paul and Silas walked out of prison as free men in 16:40—a little worse for wear physically, but absolutely full spiritually. Their interaction with Lydia at the riverside was only the beginning of their friendship, and visiting with her was a priority on their way out of the city. They also encouraged the men who had become brothers, then it was on to their next stop. But Paul didn't forget the people he met in Philippi. In fact, he wrote a letter to the church he planted there, and the recipients may have included the people he met on this stop—from Lydia to the demonized girl to the jailer and his family!

DAY 4

Acts 17:1–15

READ ACTS 17:1–15

1. On Journey Map Two (page 16), chart what we'll study in today's passage.

Review 17:1–9.

Philippians 4:15–16 says the church in Philippi financially supported Paul's time in Thessalonica. It's likely Lydia made a contribution when she bid them farewell. The walk was about a hundred miles and probably took about three days. When Paul and Silas arrived, they were true to their conviction to bring the gospel to the Jews first.

The advantage of taking their message to the Jews and God-fearing Greeks was Paul didn't need to convince them the Scriptures were true. (At this point, the only Scriptures were the Old Testament, and everyone in the room could agree on their importance.) Paul's message of Christ was not a departure from the Old Testament, but a continuation and fulfillment of it.

2. Paul's gospel presentation included four parts. **Use a Greek lexicon and Bible commentary to fill in the table below with what each section may have entailed.**

Reasoned	
Explained	
Proved	
Concluded (*saying*)	

3. What was the response from the Jews and God-fearing Greeks? Circle all that apply.

A. All of them believed.
B. A lot of Greeks believed.
C. Only men responded.
D. Many leading women believed.
E. Religious leaders who didn't believe became jealous.

Luke had some favorite phrases when it came to numbers. In this passage we see "a great many" and "not a few." They both mean "a lot"! Be on the lookout for these types of statements.

The jealous religious leaders sought out some wicked men to stir up a mob. It only took three Sabbath days for this city to go into an uproar. When this angry mob couldn't find Paul and Silas in Jason's house—likely a hub for this fledgling church—they snatched Jason and a few of the new believers.

4. What two allegations were leveled against these young Christians? How was this actually a compliment to the effectiveness of the church in the region?

The gospel of Jesus was changing entire communities by flipping individual believers' lives upside down—amending their values systems, challenging their cultural norms, and granting purpose to those on the outskirts of society—and that's still happening today. Jesus's entire kingdom message flies in the face of conventional understanding. Many even refer to it as the upside-down kingdom.

★ 5. Do you think about the gospel of Jesus as an addition to your life or as something that has completely redefined it? Explain.

We know from the Gospels and from Paul's life that the accusation of lawlessness simply wasn't true. Scripture calls believers to submit to earthly authority and to pray for their governments. The natural result of following Jesus is that we become *better* citizens of our earthly homes!

The local authorities didn't seem to care who caused the disturbance; they just wanted it to end. So Jason, the victim in this scenario, was required to pay a security deposit to ensure the mob would disperse. Perhaps Paul and Silas departed because of the nature of the agreement with the city officials, or perhaps they left to ensure Jason's deposit wouldn't be compromised.

Paul and Silas were only in Thessalonica for a few weeks (17:2) when they had to leave under the cover of night. But Paul clearly wasn't done investing in these believers. The New Testament book of 1 Thessalonians was probably Paul's first communication with them after this experience.

Review 17:10–15.

In their next stop, Berea, those gathered in the synagogue were glad to receive the message with open hearts and clear minds—unlike many of the Thessalonians. But they weren't satisfied with accepting it outright.

★ 6. **Look up the word *examining* (17:11) in a Greek lexicon and record what you find.** How is this different from simply hearing and accepting a sermon as true? Is this a regular practice in your life? Why or why not?

Paul had no reason to fear the Bereans checking his words against the Scriptures. It showed they were hungry for the truth, not just for what was popular or easy on the ears.

Word of what God was doing traveled the fifty miles back to Thessalonica, and it wasn't received well. The evil rabble-rousers arrived in Berea to stir up the crowds against the ministry and message of Christ. It wasn't enough that Paul and Silas had left their city; they wanted this influence removed from the region entirely.

Though Paul, Silas, and Timothy would eventually depart for Athens, Paul was the only one to depart under threat of the crowd. It's likely he wanted Silas and Timothy to continue to establish the church and disciple its believers. He wasn't just trying to make converts, but to establish churches for ongoing discipleship. He knew the men he had trained could handle the task in his absence. That disciples have intentionally discipled others throughout the past two thousand years has paved the way for us to know Jesus today!

7. Fill in the table below.

What was the response from each group?

Thessalonian religious Jews	Thessalonian leading women	Thessalonian God-fearing Greeks	Berean Jews	Berean Greek women of high standing	Berean Greek men of high standing

What does this say about God's heart?

DAY 5

Acts 17:16–34

 READ ACTS 17:16–34

Review 17:16–21.

Paul arrived alone in Athens, where the need for the gospel was so evident he couldn't resist beginning ministry immediately. The city's sculptures, whose craftsmanship would amaze and astonish, were repulsive to Paul. He began to reason with the Jews in the synagogue, but seemed to focus his time in Athens with those in the marketplace who were willing to engage. Athens was unlike any other city Paul had ministered in; it was a proud city full of culture and education, an intellectual and religious hub of the civilized world.

1. **Use a Bible commentary to describe the two types of philosophers who were engaging Paul.**

Epicurean	
Stoic	

The differences between these two groups of intellectuals would have regularly set them at odds. But both were intrigued—albeit maybe mockingly so—by Paul's reasoning. Even with a new audience, Paul's message had not strayed from Jesus and the resurrection. The novelty of Paul's message, not the content of it, resulted in an invitation to teach at the Areopagus, a rocky hillside where philosophical discussions and debates commonly took place.

★ 2. What were the philosophically driven Athenians consumed with pursuing? How is this similar to our society today?

Review 17:22–28.

Paul always met his audience where they were, then made a beeline for Jesus. He didn't begin his message in Athens with Scripture, because they didn't build their lives around it. Instead, Paul began by pointing out the religious investment this group of people had made. This wasn't necessarily a compliment or an insult, but an acknowledgment of his hearers' spiritual reality. The Greeks had so many gods that in order to not offend one who might have been overlooked, they created an altar with the inscription "To the unknown god."

This altar set the stage perfectly for Paul to introduce the philosophers to the one true God they had not previously known.

3. Circle all the truths about God that Paul references in his message.

A. God created and controls everything.
B. God is separate from creation.
C. God can't be fully represented by anything made by human hands.
D. God doesn't need anything from man.
E. God provides everything for man.
F. God is intentional with every life.
G. God created man with a longing to know Him.
H. God is not far away.
I. God created the dinosaurs.
J. God is not in control.

Paul covered a lot of ground quickly, so let's note a few things.

First, he spoke of life and breath and everything that humankind experiences on a daily basis. These things are true of all who live, not just believers. As we discussed on Day 3 of last week, theologians call this *common grace*. It refers to the fact that God would be within His rights to strike us dead after our first sin, but He didn't! Even those who don't know him as Savior still get to live on earth receiving non-redemptive blessings like daily breath. The existence of common grace encourages sinners to repent and believe in the saving grace offered in Christ.

Second, God has a plan for the unfolding of human history. He established where each person would be born and where they would live.

Third, God placed a yearning for Himself in the hearts of humankind—and therefore, these philosophers were not far off! They were looking for truth, just in the wrong places.

4. **Use a Bible commentary to find out who Paul quotes in 17:28.** Why do you think he quoted these people?

Review 17:29–34.

5. Summarize Paul's conclusion in 17:29–31 in your own words. **Use a Bible commentary as needed.**

Paul's argument was received with mixed results. Some mocked him, others wanted to hear more, and some joined him and believed.

★ 6. What can we learn about evangelism from this range of responses to the gospel?

Paul could meet the Athenians where they were and direct them to Jesus because God meets us right where we are. We're made to seek and know Him, and He's not far off. Dionysius, a notable figure of the Areopagus, a woman named Damaris, and others learned that day what we know to be true: He's where the joy is!

7. What stood out to you most in this week's study? Why?

8. What did you learn or relearn about God and His character this week?

DAY 6

Corresponding Psalm & Prayer

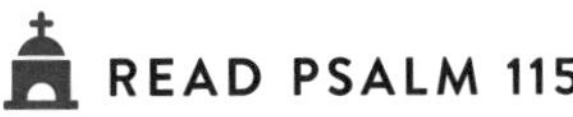

READ PSALM 115

1. What correlation do you see between Psalm 115 and this week's study?

2. What portions of this psalm stand out to you most?

3. Close by praying this prayer aloud:

Father,

You are our God. You are in the heavens, and You do all that You please. You are with us on earth, and You remember us and bless us. Forever we will praise You!

Like Paul told the Athenians, You've given each of us a desire to know You. But like the psalmist wrote, we've made our own idols and have worshiped them. We've longed for security, prosperity, and popularity instead of longing for You. By adoring things that don't see, hear, or feel, we've also failed to see, hear, and feel.

Remind me that You provide everything I need. Remind me that You're not far away. Let me see Your glory. Let me hear Your voice. Let me feel Your presence.

I surrender my life to You, Lord—every moment of my day, each decision I make, I yield my will and way to Your perfect will and way.

I love You too. Amen.

DAY 7

Rest, Catch Up, or Dig Deeper

WEEKLY CHALLENGE

On Day 4, we read about the Bereans, who received the message of the gospel with open hearts and clear minds. They were attentive to what was being preached, but they didn't take it at face value. These were people who wanted to confirm the truth for themselves before they would believe it. So they eagerly examined the Scriptures.

This week, listen to a sermon or Christian podcast and check it against Scripture for yourself. Use Bible study tools and cross references to determine whether what you hear is true. Remember that Jesus prayed we would be sanctified by truth, and that God's Word is truth (John 17:17).

WEEK 7

Scripture to Memorize

"And he commanded us to preach to the people and to testify that he is the one appointed by God to be judge of the living and the dead."

Acts 10:42

Acts 18–20

Approximate Years: AD 54–57

DAILY BIBLE READING

Day 1: Acts 18

Day 2: Acts 19:1–20

Day 3: Acts 19:21–41

Day 4: Acts 20:1–16

Day 5: Acts 20:17–38

Day 6: Psalm 85

Day 7: Catch-Up Day

Corresponds to Days 332 and 346 of *The Bible Recap.*

WEEKLY CHALLENGE

See page 193 for more information.

Acts 18

READ ACTS 18

Review 18:1–17.

In this week's study, we see Paul end his second missionary journey and begin his third.

1. On Journey Map Two (page 16), draw a line from Athens to the place Paul met Aquila and Priscilla.

The Greek city of Corinth was an important crossroads in the Roman Empire. It was a major center of trade and travel, and Paul would've known that a church planted in Corinth would impact people from all over the world. But planting a church there wouldn't be easy.

Corinth was famous for its immorality. In that day, *Corinthian companion* meant "prostitute."[1] The phrase *act like a Corinthian* referred to sexual exploits, and worship of Aphrodite, goddess of sexuality and fertility, was rampant. Amid this great challenge, God provided two new friends for Paul.

2. What do we know about Aquila and Priscilla?

A. They were porcupine traders.
B. They were tentmakers.
C. They had recently come from Italy.
D. They were Jews.
E. They were there because of an order of Claudius.
F. All but A.

In about half the mentions of this married couple in the New Testament, Priscilla's name is mentioned first, which was unusual for the time. Her name is a form of Prisca, one of the great family names of Rome.[2] It's likely she was connected to this great family. Throughout Acts, we see God used both women and men, both the well-connected and the lowly, in His plan to establish His church.

Paul, also a tentmaker, stayed with this couple and worked with them during the week. In 2 Thessalonians 3:6–12, we see what might be Paul's reasoning behind this. He desired to model for believers an example of not being a financial burden, even in ministry. Paul often chose to go the extra mile, at the expense of his own freedom. It wasn't a prescriptive model—it wasn't based on rules. To the contrary, it was a willingness to go above and beyond the minimum requirements. Fervently wishing to see the gospel spread without inhibition, he was willing to do whatever he could to remove impediments for others.

3. What did Paul do every Sabbath?

Take note of the word Luke uses: *reasoned*. We'll see it again in 18:19, and it's a reminder that Paul was not bringing mere emotional appeals—he was teaching the truth of Jesus through reason.

Silas and Timothy may have brought funding with them, because once they arrived, Paul moved from part-time tentmaking to full-time preaching. He began by sharing the Word with the Jews. But when they opposed him, he shook out his garments and turned to the Gentiles, and many Corinthians came to faith—in addition to Crispus, the synagogue ruler!

We may think of Paul as a man unbothered by setbacks and immune to discouragement.

★ 4. What do you find in 18:9–10 that may suggest otherwise?

Perhaps God saw Paul had grown weary from the harsh Corinthian environment and was encouraging him. Or perhaps God was warning him, because during his year-and-a-half stay, the Jews made a "united attack" on Paul. But before Paul even opened his mouth to respond, the Roman proconsul used reason to turn the crowd—confirming God's assurance in the vision. Here, Sosthenes is referred to as the synagogue ruler, which may mean Crispus was replaced as synagogue ruler when he became a Christian.

5. Who else eventually became a Christian, according to 1 Corinthians 1:1?

Review 18:18–23.

6. On Journey Map Two, chart Paul's journey in these verses. Be sure to take Priscilla and Aquila along, just as Paul did, and leave them in Ephesus.

Scholars aren't exactly sure what vow Paul was under, but many suggest it was the Nazirite vow (Numbers 6:1–21). He often modeled self-sacrifice for the sake of unity among believers. But considering the depravity of Corinth, this was likely a vow to set himself *apart* while he lived there. Unity with the body but distinction from the world.

Paul's return to Antioch in 18:22 ended his second missionary journey. His departure in 18:23 signaled the beginning of his third.

7. Update your timeline (page 19) to record that in the year 54, Paul's third missionary journey began.

Review 18:24–28.

8. Fill out the following personal profile on Apollos.

Ethnicity:

Hometown:

Currently living in:

Abilities:

Education:

Things he taught accurately:

Gaps in education:

This amazing speaker, fervent in spirit, was boldly teaching in Ephesus, but he needed a little guidance. If only God had sent someone ahead to explain things to him. Oh wait—He did!

★ 9. Apollos's story is such an encouragement that we don't have to know everything to speak the truth of God fervently. Have you ever been hesitant to share the gospel because you felt like you didn't know enough?

Priscilla and Aquila explained the way of God more accurately, and Apollos seemed to receive it with such eagerness and humility that, a verse later, he was ready to begin his own missionary journey! He went on to powerfully show the Jews by Scripture that Jesus was the Christ. Up to this point, we've primarily seen Paul as the one attempting to bring truth to the Jews in the synagogue—and look how God wove new people into this plan. Paul would've been the first one to agree: Acts isn't the Paul show; it's the God show. And God was showing up all over the place!

DAY 2

Acts 19:1–20

READ ACTS 19:1–20

Review 19:1–10.

Yesterday, we learned about Apollos teaching in Ephesus, then being sent off to Achaia. In today's study, Paul came to Ephesus to pick up where Apollos left off.

1. How were these new disciples like Apollos? What was the result of Paul teaching them?

In 19:8–10, we see a big shift in our Acts narrative. Up to this point, Paul had visited the synagogues first on his journeys, then taken the Word to the Gentiles—sort of a "from the synagogues to the streets" route. Here, we see Paul spoke boldly in the synagogue for three months. (Note Luke's use of the word *reasoning* again in 19:8—this gospel is not one that asks believers to check their brains at the door.)

2. Where did Paul go when they spoke evil of the Way? How long did he stay there?

This time, Paul didn't go from the synagogues to the streets. He went from the synagogue—which had very specific rules about access and who could enter—to the hall of Tyrannus, which may have been as open to the public as a rec center. Some historical documents suggest Paul spoke there daily from eleven in the morning to four in the afternoon, which was the hottest time of day, when most Ephesians would've rested from their work. And this went on daily for two years. This was basically a two-year seminary happening in the middle of one of the darkest city centers on earth!

3. Fill in the blanks from 19:10.

> "This continued for two years, so that ____ ___ ________ __ _____ heard the word of the Lord, both Jews and Greeks."

Does the mention of this region spark any memories for you from last week's study? Remember, in 16:6, Paul and his group had been "forbidden by the Holy Spirit to speak the word in Asia." We discussed that God's *no* to Paul going to Asia was more like a *not yet*.

Sometimes, God's *not yets* can be hard to understand in the moment. Romans 11:33 says the riches of God's wisdom are so deep that His paths are "beyond tracing out" (NIV). We usually can't predict the reasons for His *not yets*. But how awe-inspiring when we get the privilege of witnessing what God was up to. Paul was told no in 16:6 so that Apollos could be sent to Ephesus to lay God's groundwork, only for Paul to arrive at the perfect moment after Apollos left—that all of Asia might hear the word of the Lord.

Review 19:11–20.

Ephesus was famous for being a hotbed of witchcraft and sorcery. And here we see God again being specific and strategic in His spread of the truth that brings freedom.

★ 4. Why do you think God did "extraordinary" (or as some translations say, "unusual") miracles in this particular city?

We've discussed the power of the name of Jesus, and Philippians 2:9, which *Paul wrote*, tells us Jesus is "the name that is above every name." And here the sons of Sceva remind us of an important truth: The name of Jesus is not a magic spell or an *abracadabra*. The *name* of Jesus is the entirety of the person of Jesus Christ—His will, personality, and power. This key difference is evident in 19:13.

5. Which accurately completes what the exorcists said? "I adjure you by the Jesus . . ."

A. "whom we have a personal relationship with."
B. "whom we proclaim."
C. "whom Paul proclaims."
D. "whom our mom proclaims."

This passage may seem scary. But the key distinction is that these exorcists weren't empowered or protected by the name of Jesus, because they weren't working by the Spirit of God or proclaiming Jesus as their Lord. They were merely proclaiming that He was Paul's Lord.

6. Referencing 19:17–20, write down every action that resulted from this incident.

Many of these practitioners thought their magic came from secrecy. So it's especially profound that they weren't just confessing before God privately—they were confessing their sins out loud, communally.

★ 7. If/when you confess, is it solely to God or do you include other trusted believers? What opportunity does James 5:16 offer us?

The fifty thousand pieces of silver in 19:19 would equal $1–5 million today.[1] It's compelling to think about our financial relationships with strongholds—the million- and billion-dollar industries that keep us captive, that represent our strongholds. We'll explore that more tomorrow. But thank God the Word of the Lord continued to prevail—and it continues to prevail today.

8. Update your timeline (page 19) to note the fifth summary update on the growth of the church was recorded in 19:20.

DAY 3

Acts 19:21–41

READ ACTS 19:21–41

We're still in Ephesus, but today's study has a lot of new names.

1. Before we dive in, fill out the table below to keep track of today's players. A few blanks are filled to help get you started.

Name	Role	Action	Helped, Opposed, or Both
Timothy	Paul's helper	Sent to Macedonia	Helped
Erastus			
Demetrius	Silversmith		
Artemis		Nothing—because gods made with hands can't do anything!	
Gaius and Aristarchus			
Disciples			
Asiarchs	Men of high honorary rank in the Roman province of Asia, friends of Paul		
Ephesian crowd			
Alexander			
Town clerk			

Notice the Asiarchs are listed among Paul's friends. Throughout Acts, we see God provided Paul with well-placed people in the cities he went to. Sometimes those people were at the top of the food chain. Sometimes they were jailers or tentmakers or God-fearing, business-minded women. But we continue to see God fulfill what He spoke in 18:9–10: "Do not be afraid . . . for I have many in this city who are my people." God spoke that word to Paul in Corinth, but we see that it's also true here in Ephesus. Some of the people God appointed to help Paul spread the gospel were willing participants. And some, it seems, may have been compelled to help the cause without even knowing it.

Review 19:21–41.

Yesterday's study ended with the remarkable moment when the Ephesians burned what would've been the modern equivalent of $1–5 million dollars' worth of sorcery materials. Today, the financial ramifications of the spread of the gospel continue.

Paul, guided by the Spirit, resolved to take the journey that would eventually lead him to Rome. But about that time, a commotion erupted in Ephesus, courtesy of the tradesmen who'd made their living crafting items for the worship of the goddess Artemis, also known as Diana.

The Roman goddess Diana and the Greek goddess Artemis were combined into one goddess and cult of worship when Rome was attempting to unify and control the region's locals. This explains why you may come across mention of either Diana or Artemis in this passage, depending on the version of the Bible you're using.

★ 2. In 19:27, Demetrius mentions two motivations for his concern. What do you think his motivation actually was? Briefly explain your answer.

The Temple of Artemis in Ephesus was world-famous. The trinkets and tokens they made were big business, so it isn't hard to imagine the riot may have been economically motivated.

★ 3. What common word do you notice in 19:29 and 19:32?

Most of them didn't know why they had come together. And yet, when the crowd recognized Alexander was a Jew, they spent about two hours crying out with one voice in worship of Artemis. Don't let cultural differences tempt you to think a crowd muddled with confusion, crying out in one voice *for two hours*, is normal. Clearly, whatever motives these people had for the riot carried an undercurrent of Satan working hard against the gospel in Ephesus. Chanting in unison for five minutes would be a long time. Chanting in unison for two hours was probably as creepy and demonic as it sounds. It's no surprise that in Paul's letter to the Ephesians, we find his greatest emphasis on how to handle spiritual warfare (Ephesians 6:10–18).

4. Who ultimately calmed the crowd in 19:35?

A. Paul
B. Barnabas
C. Lydia
D. The Ephesian town clerk

Once again, God provided support for Paul in an unexpected way. The Ephesian town clerk, who didn't seem to be a believer in Jesus, used an interesting appeal on Paul's behalf. He said if Artemis was so great—great enough to chant about for two hours straight—then why should they feel threatened by Paul's gospel? He said any charge Demetrius and the craftsmen had should be raised properly in the courts.

5. According to the town clerk, what was actually illegal?

God's purposes prevail. And just like in 18:14, Paul didn't even have to open his mouth.

DAY 4

Acts 20:1–16

READ ACTS 20:1–16

Review 20:1–6.

Paul had spent over two years teaching in Ephesus and building up the disciples, but the riot signaled it was time to move on to the next destination.

1. On Journey Map Three (page 17), plot Paul's travels in 20:3–6. Draw a dotted line to show where he planned to go by sea. Draw a solid line over the land route he took instead.

2. Circle all of Paul's companions mentioned in 20:4.

- Thor the Asgardian
- Sopater the Berean
- Aristarchus the Thessalonian
- Secundus the Thessalonian
- Gaius of Derbe
- Tychicus the Asian
- Tater the Tot
- Trophimus the Asian
- Conan the Barbarian
- Timothy

These traveling companions were likely representatives from other churches, and they were a diverse group. Take note of the two from Thessalonica. Aristarchus's name refers to aristocracy, the ruling class. Secundus was a common slave name. Slaves were usually not called by their own names; the top-ranking slave in a household would be Primus, the second-ranking would be Secundus.[1] This means Secundus was a secondary citizen even among slaves. Yet, in the kingdom of God, Aristarchus and Secundus traveled side by side with Paul. In their hometown of Thessalonica, they wouldn't have been at the same table, unless Secundus was serving at it. But in the kingdom of God, they were serving *together*. One of many ways the gospel was turning this ancient world upside down.

★ 3. Why was it beneficial for Paul to have a diverse group of ministry companions on his journey? What can we learn from his example?

Next, Luke said they sailed away from Philippi after the days of Unleavened Bread (Passover), arrived at Troas in five days, and stayed there for seven. Bear that in mind, because we'll be circling back.

Review 20:7–16.

This is one of the places in Scripture where we see the early church gathering on the first day of the week to break bread, fellowship, and be in the Word. But this was no ordinary church service.

4. What time markers in 20:7 and 20:11 give you a sense of how long Paul preached and talked with them? Draw the approximate times on the clocks below.

This echoes the sense of urgency Jesus displayed during the Upper Room Discourse on the night before His arrest (John 13–17); and even then, His exhausted disciples kept falling asleep. Clearly, in urgent moments, God does not rule out all-nighters. Paul knew he'd be leaving them the next morning, and his heart for discipleship is evident here. Notice in 20:7, he "talked with them," and then there was a "speech." Later in 20:11, he "conversed with them a long while." There was a combination of preaching and relational engagement. He taught, and then they talked about it together the rest of the night. He invested in them. Between all that, a young man was raised from the dead.

5. What happened after Eutychus was brought back to life?

A. They called it a day.
B. They broke bread and ate.
C. They continued their meeting, talking until daybreak.
D. They were "not a little comforted."
E. All but A.

Luke once again employed one of his favorite literary devices: understatement. They were "not a little comforted." No doubt.

★ 6. Why do you think Luke included this story in his account of their time in Troas?

After Eutychus was raised from the dead, Luke and the others sailed to Assos, where they picked up Paul, who came by land to meet them.

7. On Journey Map Three, plot Paul's boat journey from Assos to Miletus. Keep your eye on Jerusalem, bearing in mind Paul's desire to arrive there by Pentecost.

Pentecost is fifty days after the Feast of Unleavened Bread. Using the mention of the five and seven days passing in 20:6, and the handful of days devoted to sea travel in 20:13–16, we might guess there were about thirty-two days remaining until Pentecost at this point in Paul's journey. But if you're concerned about the Ephesians being skipped in Paul's haste to get to Jerusalem, don't worry. As we'll see in tomorrow's study, God has a plan. He always does.

DAY 5

Acts 20:17–38

READ ACTS 20:17–38

Review Acts 20:17–38.

Today's study opens with Paul in Miletus, sending word to the Ephesian church leaders to meet with him. He may have done this because, though he wanted to spend time with them, he knew a trip to Ephesus wouldn't be a short one.

1. What do you think was Paul's motivation for what he said in 20:18–21?

   A. Bragging
   B. Lowkey bragging
   C. Correcting their wrong ideas about him
   D. Modeling and teaching

Many times, Paul was required to stand before accusers or persuade an opponent, but here, he was speaking to friends, to his flock. He was reminding them of the way they'd seen him live, reminding them to do likewise, reminding them of the tears and trials he suffered so that they might hear the gospel and grow in it. He wasn't looking for a thank-you. He was handing them the baton. He knew he wouldn't see them again.

2. In 20:20, where does Paul mention teaching them?

   ". . . in public and ____ ______ ___ ______ . . ."

Though we've been referring to the "Ephesian church," there was no central church location. These churches Paul was planting were largely collections of home churches. Each elder at this meeting may have been a leader of a home church. Collectively, this fellowship of people who met in homes throughout the city would think of themselves as the Ephesian church. It's a reminder for us, who are accustomed to the idea of church being a building. Church is a body—a body of believers, united in Christ. And whether that body meets in a house, on a ship, in a cathedral, or by the river, Christ is the foundation it stands on.

3. In 20:22–23, Paul spoke about his future. What did he know for sure, and what did he not know?

It's possible that Paul knew he would be killed as far back as his conversion in Acts 9. God alluded to it in His conversation with Ananias. Even if Paul was aware of his coming execution, however, there was still a lot he *didn't* know. There were things God revealed to him, and there were things Paul had to step into in blind faith and trust—just like we do.

Paul didn't die until many years after this talk with the Ephesians, but he clearly had his death in mind. How did he wrap his head around his coming execution? He said he did not count his life worth any value beyond how it allowed him to testify to the gospel.

★ 4. Is the gospel you preach worth dying for?

You may notice the tone in this passage feels different from some of the teaching and preaching we've seen from Paul so far in Acts. The personal, relational quality of these verses reminds us of the Pauline letters we find later in the New Testament. Earlier in Acts, we were watching Paul teach the gospel to unbelieving nations that had never heard it. Here, we're watching him nurture the gospel seed that has already been planted. So his tone is both encouraging *and* challenging.

5. What did he warn them of in 20:29? And from where will the "men speaking twisted things" arise in 20:30?

Up to this point, the emphasis was on outside oppression. The Jewish leaders, the Romans, the Gentiles who opposed them—all of these were people early church believers had to be on their guard against. But now that the church was established and growing, Paul warned them it would get more complicated. The wolves would come from *among them*.

6. How does Paul begin 20:31?

"______________ ____ ________, ___________ that for three years I did not cease night or day to admonish every one with tears."

Keep an eye out for Paul's *therefores*. He often reminded listeners of truths that he would then connect with a call to respond.

★ 7. Based on the example he reminded them of in 20:31–34, what response do you think he was compelling them to live out in 20:35?

Recall what the Ephesians were like when Paul first arrived, and marvel at the impact the gospel made on them by the time they said goodbye to Paul! God is *truly* a God of transformation. And He's where the joy is!

8. What stood out to you most in this week's study? Why?

9. What did you learn or relearn about God and His character this week?

DAY 6

Corresponding Psalm & Prayer

READ PSALM 85

1. What correlation do you see between Psalm 85 and this week's study?

2. What portions of this psalm stand out to you most?

3. Close by praying this prayer aloud:

Father,

You speak peace and You give what is good. You made us, You saved us, and You love us.

Before Your apostles went anywhere, You went before them. You made a way. You guided their steps. Before I go anywhere, You've already gone before me. You've made a way. You will guide my steps. But instead of asking for Your guidance, I've relied on myself to find my own way. Choosing my own path has led to destruction.

Before Your apostles spoke about You, You gave them Your words. You created knowledge and understanding, and You give wisdom when we ask. You use those gifts through us to bring others to Yourself. But I'm arrogant enough to credit myself for Your work. Forgive me, Lord.

Let me not turn back to folly. Revive me, so that I may rejoice in You. Show me Your steadfast love.

I surrender my life to You, Lord—every moment of my day, each decision I make, I yield my will and way to Your perfect will and way.

I love You too. Amen.

DAY 7

Rest, Catch Up, or Dig Deeper

WEEKLY CHALLENGE

This week's study continued to show the detailed ways God went before Paul in his travels to provide for him and prepare the way. Make a timeline of your own life, marking moments when you can see how God prepared people, places, and things for you in advance. Maybe they're things that specifically led you to a calling or work. Maybe they're relationships that ended up being much more significant than you first imagined. Feel free to use drawings and pictures if you want to get creative. And don't assume you already know what the answers are—invite God to reveal His providence to you in ways you haven't realized before!

WEEK 8

Acts 21–23

Approximate Year: AD 58

Scripture to Memorize

"To him all the prophets bear witness that everyone who believes in him receives forgiveness of sins through his name."

Acts 10:43

DAILY BIBLE READING

Day 1: Acts 21:1–26

Day 2: Acts 21:27–40

Day 3: Acts 22:1–29

Day 4: Acts 22:30–23:11

Day 5: Acts 23:12–35

Day 6: Psalm 23

Day 7: Catch-Up Day

Corresponds to Day 346 of *The Bible Recap*.

WEEKLY CHALLENGE

See page 216 for more information.

DAY 1

Acts 21:1–26

 READ ACTS 21:1–26

Review 21:1–6.

Paul completed his last missionary journey and was making his way to Jerusalem. Each of the stops mentioned was most likely brief—no more than one day in each port.

1. Mark the route on Journey Map Three (page 17).

In Tyre, a coastal city about one hundred miles north of Jerusalem, Paul and his companions stayed with the disciples.

★ 2. **Revisit 20:22–23 and compare it with 21:4.** Write down what you notice below. Do these passages seem contradictory? Why or why not?

It seems a few different things are happening here. It's important to note that Paul was convinced the Spirit was directing him to go to Jerusalem. This was confirmed by the Spirit, who told the believers in Tyre about dangers awaiting Paul. Scholars suggest that rather than contradicting what Paul had been told, the believers were expressing their concern for Paul's safety. The Spirit had alerted both Paul and the believers that trouble awaited

Paul, yet they responded differently. Paul's friends cared about his safety. No doubt this concerned Paul as well, but he cared more about completing his ministry and testifying about the good news wherever he was called.

Paul had previously fled from danger and persecution. It wasn't that he had a death wish. But he knew the Holy Spirit was sending him to Jerusalem. The disciples, including their wives and children, prayed together with Paul and his companions and sent him away, knowing they might never see him again.

Review 21:7–16.

The journey continued from Tyre to Ptolemais and onto Caesarea. The group stayed with Philip—now nicknamed "the evangelist" because of his ministry in Acts 8.

3. Who else is mentioned in 21:9? What does Luke say about them?

Although it was highly unusual for the time, Luke made a common practice of highlighting the women involved in the church. The mention of Philip's daughters here is no exception. People previously on the outskirts of society were given equal value in the church.

A prophet named Agabus came from Judea to Caesarea—perhaps to relay this message to Paul. This is the third confirmation from the Spirit that trouble awaited Paul in Jerusalem.

4. Fill in the table below:

What did Agabus say?	How did the people respond?	How did Paul respond?

Paul was not to be deterred. Despite the high emotions within the group—including Paul's—he knew what he needed to do. The final consensus from the believers placed the situation back where it belonged—in the hands of the Lord, according to His will. This could have been a moment of division and disagreement among the believers. But instead, they appealed to the sovereignty of God, trusting in His plan. Paul would go to Jerusalem.

Review 21:17–26.

When Paul reached Jerusalem, he met with James and the elders of the church. He shared about the incredible work of God among the Gentiles, and the leaders responded by glorifying God. But Paul quickly learned of a potential problem with his visit: He didn't have the best reputation in the eyes of the most zealous Jewish Christians in Jerusalem.

5. According to 21:21, what had some people said about Paul?

6. What advice did the leaders give him?

7. Circle what Paul did in response to the elders' request:

He got upset and left Jerusalem immediately.

He did what they asked him to do.

He confronted the Jewish Christians who misrepresented him.

It seemed like Paul—despite being a Christian living under grace—was still abiding by the law. This was about eight years after the Jerusalem Council (Acts 15). Although some things in the church were crystal clear—Jesus is the Son of God and He rose from the dead—there were other things they were still figuring out. And in that environment, Paul always presented himself as a person willing to sacrifice his personal freedoms for the greater good of spreading the gospel. Considering the incredible cultural and religious divide that separated the Jews and Gentiles for centuries, the church's persistent pursuit of unity was respectable.

★ 8. **Read 1 Corinthians 9:19–23.** Write down what stands out to you based on the decision Paul made in this story.

Paul most likely wrote his letter to the Corinthians after this event in Jerusalem. Perhaps he had this experience in mind when he wrote. Paul displayed humility in acquiescing to the request of the church leaders in Jerusalem. He had just shared with them all God did among the Gentiles *through* his ministry. He didn't concern himself with defending his reputation or setting the record straight. Instead, he did what was best for the church in Jerusalem and the continued spread of the gospel. Paul limited his earthly freedom so that other people might find eternal freedom.

DAY 2

Acts 21:27–40

Review 21:27–36.

Paul was in the temple to purify himself on the final day of his vow. The leaders of the Jerusalem church hoped Paul's public observance of the law might distill the tension.

But the Jews from Asia had a different idea.

These Asian Jews were most likely from Ephesus—where there had also been a major disturbance. We don't know why they were in Jerusalem—perhaps they were there for Pentecost—but we do know they reacted to Paul's presence in the temple by stirring up the crowd.

1. Check the box next to the accusations made against Paul.

- ☐ He taught against the people.
- ☐ He taught against the law.
- ☐ He taught against this place (the temple).
- ☐ He brought a Greek into the temple.
- ☐ He defiled this holy place.

★ 2. Do any of these remind you of accusations made against Stephen in Acts 6?

These Jews assumed Paul brought his friend Trophimus, a Gentile from Ephesus, into the main area of the temple. If Paul had done this—which he had not—he would have broken their laws about defiling the temple. According to Jewish law, the Gentiles were only allowed in a specific area.

3. Look at the picture of the temple below and mark where Gentiles were permitted.

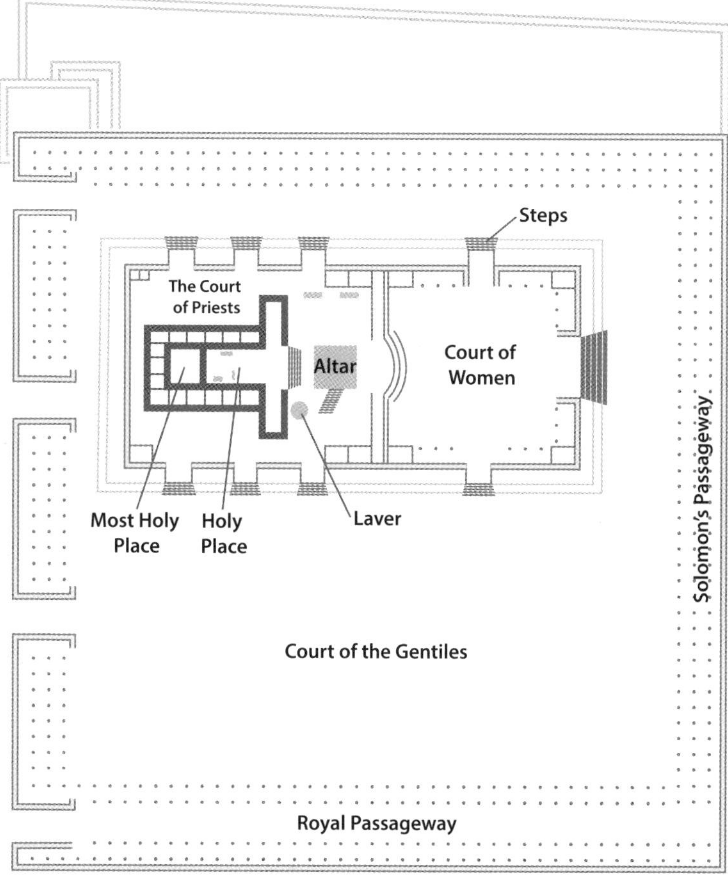

Luke first introduced us to Paul at the end of Acts 7. We met him as an enemy of the believers—a man consumed with destroying the Way. But we saw his conversion and subsequent introduction to ministry in Acts 9 and 11. We followed his missionary journeys from Acts 13 onward, noting the persecution and suffering as well as the joys of seeing the gospel spread to both Jews and Gentiles.

★ 4. Imagine you are Paul's lawyer. Based on what you know about Paul from your study of Acts, how would you dispute these accusations?

Unfortunately, these Jews from Asia weren't interested in bringing Paul to trial. Chaos ensued as the crowd seized Paul, dragged him out of the temple, and sought to kill him. Word of the situation made its way to the Roman tribune. This Roman military officer of high rank—we'll learn later that his name is Claudius Lysias (23:26)—was in charge of about one thousand soldiers, and some scholars suggest he brought close to two hundred men with him to the scene.

5. What were the crowds doing to Paul when the tribune finally arrived?

The tribune arrested Paul and attempted to learn who he was and what he had done. But the situation proved too tumultuous for the tribune to get the information he needed. The people became so unruly that Paul had to be carried off by the soldiers for his own safety.

6. Update your timeline (page 19) to record that in the year 58, Paul was arrested in Jerusalem.

Review 21:37–40.

Paul was a polyglot. He spoke at least Greek, Aramaic, and Hebrew—perhaps other languages as well—much to the surprise of the Roman tribune. Based on the tribune's response to Paul, it's likely he assumed the situation at the temple was another Jewish uprising. Josephus, a first-century Jewish historian, wrote about this Egyptian man and the revolt in his book *Of The War, Book II*. This revolt would've taken place only a few years prior.

Although the tribune couldn't get the facts from the crowds, Paul could at least clarify who he was and where he was from. He asked the tribune if he could address the crowd. Given the tribune's desire to understand the situation, he was probably happy to let Paul speak. Maybe he would finally figure out what Paul had done wrong. Good luck with that!

DAY 3

Acts 22:1–29

READ ACTS 22:1–29

Review 22:1–11.

Paul began his speech to the crowd—who had just beaten him and hoped to kill him—with noteworthy words: "Brothers and fathers." Perhaps it was his tone or that he spoke to them in Hebrew, but they quieted down to listen to his defense.

1. Write down what we learn about Paul in 22:3.

Paul established a few points of similarity with the crowd. He was a fellow Jew, educated in Jerusalem, and he had been zealous for God—just like they had been. Paul reminded them that he'd even persecuted the Way. His statement in 22:5 implied there might have been some in the crowd—the high priest and council of elders—who would remember him, even though approximately twenty years had passed.

2. Write down the two questions Paul asked Jesus on the road to Damascus.

Did you notice that Paul referred to Jesus as Lord (Master) twice? Despite all Paul didn't know at the time of his first encounter with Jesus, he set a precedent for how he would live: obedient to the Lord, in complete submission to God's plan and purpose.

3. Fill in the blanks of 22:10b.

> And the Lord said to me, "__________, and ______ into Damascus, and there you will be ________ all that is ____________ for you _____ ________."

God had plans for Paul—we've seen that so clearly throughout Acts—but He didn't tell him everything right away. In fact, Paul was simply told the first step. But God also gave Paul the assurance that He had things appointed for him to do.

Review 22:12–16.

This is the second time we've read about Paul's conversion but the first time in Acts we've seen him publicly share the experience. He had probably recounted it numerous times before, but in this account, Paul shared some additional information. One of the most awe-inspiring things he mentioned was a nod to the abundant generosity of God in choosing him for salvation. Think of the wickedness of Paul's life at the moment God saved him. He was on his way to murder Christians for their faith in Jesus. *And yet* this was the very moment when God met him on the path and saved him. This serves as an encouraging reminder that our salvation is not based on our righteousness, but on the righteousness of Christ and the generous plan of the Father!

★ 4. **Revisit 9:17–19.** Write down anything newfound in 22:12–16. Do you think Paul's Jewish audience had any influence on what or how he shared?

Review 22:17–21.

This event in Jerusalem took place shortly after Paul's conversion, but Luke didn't mention it in 9:26–30. Paul shared that all those years ago, the Jews—some of whom might be in today's crowd—hadn't accepted his testimony. He hoped things would be different this time, but in one simple sentence he sent the crowd into another uproar: "Go, for I will send you far away to the Gentiles."

Review 22:22–29.

What made the Jews so furious when Paul mentioned his calling to the Gentiles? Throughout the Old Testament, God had consistently spoken about His desire that all people know Him—and that included the Gentiles. But Israel consistently failed at welcoming outsiders and often rejected God in the process. When Jesus spoke in the synagogue in Nazareth, He addressed God's care for Gentiles, highlighting a few Old Testament stories. Unfortunately, He received the same response from the crowds.

★ 5. **Read Luke 4:24–30 and write down the similarities between the crowds' reactions to Jesus and Paul.**

Remember the tribune Claudius? He had been patiently waiting while Paul gave a speech in a language Claudius probably didn't know. When the crowd erupted again, Claudius decided to flog Paul in hopes of getting to the bottom of this chaotic situation.

Paul took this moment to casually mention he was a Roman citizen, which meant what the officials were about to do was illegal. So far, the assumptions the tribune had made about Paul were wrong, and this one could've gotten him into a lot of trouble. The simple contrast between the Roman official (who bought his citizenship) and Paul (who was born a citizen) reveals God's sovereignty at work once again. God had a plan for Paul's life, and something as simple as where he was born was an important part of that plan!

DAY 4

Acts 22:30–23:11

READ ACTS 22:30–23:11

Review 22:30–23:5.

Once again the tribune attempted to understand what was happening between Paul and the Jews. Claudius ordered the chief priests and the council—a group of Jewish religious leaders made up of Pharisees, Sadducees, and other teachers of the law—to meet. He was determined to understand the Jews' accusations. Make note of Claudius's dilemma, as this theme will continue for the rest of the book. Paul was under Roman authority—arrested by the tribune—but this Roman official didn't know what Paul had done wrong.

1. Fill in the blanks in Paul's opening line (23:1).

"____________, I have lived ____ __________ before ________ in all good

______________ up to this ________."

Paul was not perfect. Despite his close relationship with Jesus, Paul still sinned—as we all do while we live on this earth. Yet Paul could confidently say before the Jewish religious leaders that he had lived in good conscience before God.

2. Based on Paul's character, his decisions, and his teachings, do you agree with his statement? Why or why not? Write down specific verse references.

★ 3. Is this something you can confidently say about your own life before God? If not, what needs to change?

Paul's claim clearly didn't sit well with Ananias, the high priest. He ordered Paul to be struck on the mouth. Remember how the Jews accused Paul of teaching against the law? Once again Luke wanted us to see that Paul knew and revered the law. It's the religious leaders who were in the wrong. Paul called Ananias a "whitewashed wall." This phrase alluded to an appearance of cleanliness to hide the true defilement underneath. This is reminiscent of Jesus's response to the religious leaders who opposed Him (Matthew 23:27).

Paul's forceful retort brought immediate rebuke from the council because Paul had insulted the high priest. This was against Jewish law. Scholars have different opinions about Paul's reaction in 23:5—some find it hard to believe Paul didn't recognize the high priest, and some suggest Paul's mistake was due to bad eyesight. (Note: Some scholars who believe Paul had bad eyesight propose that it was the "thorn" in his flesh he wrote about in 2 Corinthians. This could be why he wrote so large in his letter to the Galatians, and perhaps poor eyesight was a lasting effect from his blindness on the road to Damascus. See Acts 9:1–19; 2 Corinthians 12:7–10; Galatians 4:15, 6:11–18.) Regardless of the reason, Paul responded with humility, acknowledging his mistake.

Review 23:6–10.

4. Paul was a master of one-liners. What did he say that caused immediate chaos in the room?

5. Put a check next to what the Pharisees and Sadducees believe. **Use a Bible study tool if you need help.**

Pharisees

- ☐ There is resurrection
- ☐ There are angels
- ☐ There are spirits
- ☐ Jesus was resurrected

Sadducees

- ☐ There is no resurrection
- ☐ There are no angels
- ☐ There are no spirits
- ☐ Paul could be right

Once again, the scene devolved into chaos and confusion. Not only did the Jews have no valid accusations against Paul, but they turned on each other and, ironically, the Pharisees seemed to switch sides. They came to Paul's defense in 23:9. The situation quickly grew violent, and Paul was removed immediately so he wouldn't be "torn to pieces."

Sorry, Claudius. Today's not the day you figure this out!

6. **Review 23:11.** What stands out to you in this verse?

Throughout Scripture, God repeatedly tells His people "fear not," "do not be afraid," and "take courage." It's likely Paul experienced a variety of emotions as he waited in the barracks—perhaps fear and uncertainty overwhelmed him. Don't forget that Paul was human just like we are. But God stood by Paul in the barracks. He told him the next step: Paul would testify in Rome. Despite all that Paul had been through, the intensity level seemed to be rising. He would need courage for what lay ahead of him. God reminded Paul that He had a plan and He was near. God stood by Paul in Jerusalem, and He would stand by him until the end.

Acts 23:12–35

Review 23:12–22.

God just told Paul he would testify in Rome, but the Jews must not have gotten the message. They made a plan to kill Paul and even took an oath to abstain from food and drink until they accomplished their goal. These men were determined to rid themselves of Paul once and for all. Fortunately for Paul, God's plans are never thwarted.

1. Who told Paul about this plan?

This is the first time we see Paul's family mentioned. They lived in Jerusalem, and perhaps they had become believers through Paul's own conversion and testimony, though the text doesn't say for sure. The fact that Paul's nephew could visit him in prison points to Claudius's belief in Paul's innocence. Despite all that Claudius still didn't know, he had determined Paul was not a threat to Rome.

2. Note the actions of and details about each of these people in this story.

Paul's nephew:

Paul:

Centurion:

Tribune:

3. What do you notice about the response of the Roman officials?

Paul knew God had plans for him in Rome. He could be confident he wouldn't die by the hands of the Jews in Jerusalem. Still, he used wisdom in relaying the information to the Romans to ensure his safety. Paul was hated by "his brothers and fathers" (22:1). They wanted him dead. And Rome, generally considered an enemy of the Jews, provided Paul safety from his own people.

Review 23:23–35.

4. Update your timeline (page 19) to record that in the year 58†, Paul was taken to (and then held in) Caesarea.

5. Circle the people commanded to accompany Paul to Caesarea.

Two hundred soldiers	Two hundred spearmen
Seventy horsemen	Untrained Roman soldiers
His nephew	The high priest

God used 470 men in the Roman military to ensure Paul's safety as he traveled to Caesarea, which was about sixty miles away. He was even given a mount (a horse, donkey, or mule), which would provide a faster means of escape if the group was attacked.

Claudius Lysias—the full name of the tribune—wrote a letter to Felix, the governor of Caesarea, informing him of Paul's situation. Although Claudius took the opportunity to boast about saving Paul from the Jews, neglecting to mention the near-flogging incident (22:24), he also made an important statement in 23:29.

★ 6. In your own words, write down Claudius's verdict regarding Paul.

The soldiers accompanied Paul to Antipatris, about halfway to Caesarea, ensuring his safety during the most treacherous part of the journey. Reaching Antipatris with no problems, the seventy horsemen took Paul for the remainder of the journey.

Paul was presented to Felix, who inquired about his hometown. This was a standard question in Roman legal proceedings to determine where a case should be tried. Rather than sending Paul all the way to Cilicia, Felix confirmed the trial would be held in Caesarea. Paul waited for his accusers in Herod's praetorium. The praetorium was formerly Herod the Great's palace, which Rome had turned into their regional headquarters.

★ 7. **Reread 20:22–23 and read 2 Corinthians 4:16–18.** Write down any key words or phrases that correlate to Paul's current situation.

Paul probably wrote 2 Corinthians on his third missionary journey, before the events we've just read about. And Paul knew even before setting foot in Jerusalem he would experience "imprisonment and afflictions." He had suffered and he would continue to suffer for the sake of Jesus and the gospel. But Paul also lived with eternity in mind, certain of the hope he had in Jesus Christ. Jesus met Paul on the road to Damascus, He saved him, and He stood by him. No matter what Paul faced, with God by his side he knew this for certain: He's where the joy is!

8. What stood out to you most in this week's study? Why?

9. What did you learn or relearn about God and His character this week?

DAY 6

Corresponding Psalm & Prayer

READ PSALM 23

1. What correlation do you see between Psalm 23 and this week's study?

2. What portions of this psalm stand out to you most?

3. Close by praying this prayer aloud:

Father,

You reign as King, and You lead us as Shepherd. You're majestic over all the earth, yet You're still attentive to each of our needs. Even our enemies' worst plans and harshest attacks can't change Your plans. Nothing has and nothing will stop Your promises.

I try to justify my place in Your kingdom by giving myself points for good works. I strive to earn my way into Your flock by being brave enough or bold enough. Forgive me. Remind me that my salvation is not bought by my own righteousness, but was bought by Your righteousness. Remind me that You offer me rest.

You led David to rest and to restoration. You stood by Paul and reminded him You were with him. I know You're with me too, and You'll sustain me. Because of who You are, I have everything I need. Because of Your promises, I have nothing to fear.

Show me who You are, Lord.

Show me what I should do, Lord.

I surrender my life to You, Lord—every moment of my day, each decision I make, I yield my will and way to Your perfect will and way.

I love You too. Amen.

DAY 7

Rest, Catch Up, or Dig Deeper

 **WEEKLY CHALLENGE**

On Day 3, Paul recounted two questions he'd asked God: "Who are you, Lord?" and "What shall I do, Lord?"

This week, spend at least twenty minutes journaling what comes to mind when you read these two prompts.

Who are you, Lord?

What shall I do, Lord?

WEEK 9

Acts 24–26

Approximate Years: AD 58–60

Scripture to Memorize

While Peter was still saying these things, the Holy Spirit fell on all who heard the word.

Acts 10:44

DAILY BIBLE READING

Day 1: Acts 24
Day 2: Acts 25:1–12
Day 3: Acts 25:13–27
Day 4: Acts 26:1–11
Day 5: Acts 26:12–32
Day 6: Psalm 3
Day 7: Catch-Up Day

Corresponds to Day 347 of *The Bible Recap.*

WEEKLY CHALLENGE

See page 243 for more information.

Acts 24

READ ACTS 24

Paul waited at Caesarea for his accusers, the leaders of the Jews, to arrive for his trial. He was essentially being passed around as a political chess piece from one Roman official to another. Not knowing what to do with someone who had committed no crimes worthy of capital punishment, the Romans went along with the charade of these trials, all to appease the Jewish leaders.

Review 24:1–9.

Note: You may have a Bible that omits 24:7. Some, but not all, early manuscripts exclude this verse; therefore some, but not all, translations exclude it as well.

1. What tactic did Tertullus use to get on Felix's good side?

While this would've summoned a collective eyeroll from any onlooker, it was a common practice in Roman court proceedings. The prosecutor would seek favor by flattery before presenting their arguments. What makes Tertullus's comments all the more painful is how outright false they were.

Felix was known as an immoral, brutal, violent, and altogether unwise man. Tertullus's strategic disregard for the truth remained the theme of his prosecution.

2. List Tertullus's accusations against Paul. Next to each accusation, list any evidence that supports it.

Accusation	Proof

Never let the truth get in the way of a good story, right? Tertullus knew as well as the rest of the Jews that Paul had done nothing to deserve being on trial. In fact, the Jews never wanted him to be on trial. They just wanted him dead.

Review 24:10–13.

3. Why do you think Paul was so relaxed about making his defense before Felix?

During his defense, Paul used words like *verify* (24:11), *find* (24:12), and *prove* (24:13)—words Tertullus couldn't match in official court proceedings. With little effort, Paul was able to poke massive holes in Tertullus's argument.

Review 24:14–21.

Paul outlined the things he *could* be found "guilty" of, laying out what it looked like to be a follower of Jesus. Decades into this movement, Paul still referred to it as "the Way." Perhaps because Jesus had referred to Himself as the way (John 14:6). Or perhaps because Paul knew that being a believer, a true disciple of Christ, is more than just talk. True repentance and discipleship always results in a new way of life.

4. List the spiritual disciplines Paul outlined.

Notice that Paul's desire was to live with a clear conscience before both God and man (24:16). Tertullus said Paul was a "plague" to the people. Paul's good reputation was certainly valuable in defending himself against such accusations, but to him, living with a clear conscience was just part of being a disciple of Jesus.

★ 5. Are there times when you find it difficult to live with a clear conscience before man? Why?

Paul calls out the real reason he is on trial in 24:21. He may have been on trial for alleged insurrection, but what the Jews really held against him was his belief in the resurrection of Jesus. The Romans were less likely to put him to death over belief in the resurrection—that was a Jewish problem, not a Roman problem. If the Jews wanted Paul killed legally, they needed something that struck the heart of the empire.

Review 24:22–27.

Despite his reputation for poor leadership, even Felix saw how weak Tertullus's argument was and decided to put the trial off until Lysias could come to Caesarea.

6. What kindness does Felix impart to Paul while he is kept in custody?

Paul would've been entirely dependent on friends to bring him provisions—a courtesy that wasn't always extended to Roman prisoners. Even in these circumstances, the hand of God was on Paul, equipping him with all he needed to serve as God's chosen instrument.

7. List the three points of Paul's message to Felix and his wife, Drusilla. How did Felix respond to this message?

★ 8. Why do you think the message of righteousness, self-control, and judgment was difficult for Felix to hear?

Apart from knowing the saving grace of Jesus, this is a difficult message for anyone to hear. Without Christ, our righteousness is as filthy rags (Isaiah 64:6). Without the Holy Spirit, we're left to white-knuckle our way into a life of self-control (Galatians 5:22–23). Without God's mercy, we could never triumph over judgment (James 2:13). That is why all Paul's hope was in the resurrection.

Felix's discussions with Paul continued over the final two years of his reign as governor. But like Roman leaders who had come before him, Felix sought to please the Jewish crowd and left Paul in prison.

DAY 2

Acts 25:1–12

READ ACTS 25:1–12

After Paul's trial in front of Felix, two years passed before a new governor, Porcius Festus, assumed office in Caesarea. In an effort to understand the state of the union, Festus paid a visit to Jerusalem.

Review 25:1–5.

1. What was the first issue the Jews brought before Festus?

2. What favor did they ask of Festus? Why?

Take a moment to consider the situation: These were religious leaders—strict followers of the Torah—who were so overcome with hatred for Paul that they'd apparently spent the last two years plotting how they could trick the government, ambush Paul, and commit murder. This is the result when zeal for religion is separated from zeal for Christ.

★ 3. What do you think led to the Jews' extreme hatred for Paul and all he stood for?

Festus either saw through their plan or saw no need to transport Paul when he would be back in Caesarea himself in a short time. Paul's case must have been a bit puzzling for Festus. Why had Felix left Paul sitting on death row? He hadn't been sentenced. A decision had not been made concerning his freedom. He was just in prison limbo.

Review 25:6–8.

When Festus returned to Caesarea, he wasted no time in opening the case concerning Paul. This was a repeat of what Paul had already gone through with Felix. His defense was likely more lengthy in the actual trial; Luke's brevity here seems to indicate this whole affair was essentially the same story, different day.

4. Fill in the blanks concerning the accusations against Paul in 25:7.

"... bringing many and serious charges against him that they ______ ______ ________."

But if we wonder how Paul remained patient and faithful under such frustrating circumstances, we need to look no further than Paul's letters to see a greater picture. The English translation of the Greek word *tribunal* in 25:6 is *bēma*—which can also be translated as "judgment seat."

5. **Look up Romans 14:10 and 2 Corinthians 5:10.** Before whose tribunal/judgment seat/bema will all believers stand one day?

This is why Paul could remain steadfast as he faced threats from religious elites, defended himself before Roman governors, and was pelted with stones, flogged by soldiers, thrown in jail, and accused wrongly by ignorant leaders—he knew he must remain faithful to a greater Judge. All earthly judgment seats paled in comparison to the throne of God, where Paul now worships as a free, healed, pardoned son of the King.

★ 6. How does this encourage you to remain steadfast in a world of increasingly harsher judgments toward Christians?

Review 25:9–12.

Festus, despite the lack of evidence against Paul, succumbed to the same pressures his predecessor did.

7. **Compare 24:27 with 25:9.** What phrase (motive) shows up in both verses?

Even though Rome wasn't a democracy, there was significant pressure to appease their subjects to prevent an uprising. Roman leaders were the head of the empire, but in many cases, some Jews of the region would act as the neck that turned the Roman head.

8. What offer did Festus give to Paul?

Once again, we see that Rome didn't know what to do with Paul. As a leader whose primary goal was to keep the peace, Festus was caught between a rock—actual justice—and a hard place—appeasing the Jews. He just wanted to wash his hands of Paul altogether.

Paul seemed to be the only one willing to adhere to the letter of the law. Notice what he said in 25:11. If Paul were, in fact, guilty of civil crimes, he knew serving his sentence would be the right thing to do, even if that meant punishment by death. There was just one problem: He was innocent!

Paul was no fool. He knew accepting the offer to go back to Jerusalem would essentially be writing his own death certificate. So he invoked an element of Roman jurisprudence called *provocatio*;[1] it was his right as a citizen of Rome to appeal to Caesar. At this time, the Roman Caesar was the infamous Nero, one of the most corrupt leaders in the history of Rome—yet still a better option for Paul than Jerusalem.

DAY 3

Acts 25:13–27

 READ ACTS 25:13–27

Review 25:13.

Though he is not identified as Herod, Luke introduced us to yet another Herod in his account. Here, we met Herod Agrippa II. His father was the Herod who had James killed in Acts 12. Unlike his father, he was not a brutal, violent leader. However, his moral compass didn't exactly point due north.

1. Who did you presume Bernice to be?

You might be shocked to learn Bernice was King Agrippa's sister. Historians disagree on the nature of their relationship. Some say it was incestuous, while others think they were simply companions.

Review 25:14–22.

Two things we do know about Agrippa are that he was a Roman king and he was Jewish. In fact, one of the responsibilities delegated to him was to appoint the high priest of Jerusalem.

2. Based on his background, heritage, and position, what makes Agrippa a fitting person to hear Paul's case?

3. Rewrite 25:18 in your own words below.

Here we go again. If this narrative is starting to feel like a broken record, that's likely by design. As we've seen before, Luke sometimes uses repetition to drive home a point. While we might be inclined to take this situation lightly, it's important to remember Paul wasn't facing some small, insignificant charge. This wasn't a dispute over a traffic ticket. Under no uncertain terms, his accusers were seeking the death penalty. Nothing less.

★ 4. Based on 25:19, what do you perceive to be Festus's level of familiarity with Jesus?

By this time, the Christians had made a name for themselves. The phrase *no little disturbance* appears more than once in Acts because these followers of "a certain Jesus" had caused quite a ruckus—even "turned the world upside down" (17:6). So why did Festus seem to know so little about

Jesus? That question may be the greater reason Paul is on trial. (Put a pin in that; we'll come back to it tomorrow.)

Review 25:23.

5. What comes to mind when you picture a king entering a room "with great pomp"?

★ 6. Compare that to what Paul's entry might have looked like.

The world at that time saw great importance in men like Agrippa. He was powerful. He was wealthy. Everywhere he went, people made much ado about him—*and* his sister/friend/et cetera. Then there was Paul. Most people on the scene likely saw him as a nobody or as a menace to society.

7. History pop quiz! List a few major facts you know about the apostle Paul. Resist the urge to do a web search; just go with what you know.

8. Now list a few major facts you know about Herod Agrippa II.

Agrippa is not a well-known figure worldwide or in pop culture, and he left no notable legacy.

Paul, on the other hand, is arguably one of the most well-known names in Christendom. He wrote more of the New Testament than any of its other authors. His words have been published in more than 1,500 languages. He traveled across continents and cultures, leading an untold number of souls to Christ. And the list goes on.

As Paul put it, "Consider your calling, brothers: not many of you were wise according to worldly standards, not many were powerful, not many were of noble birth. But God chose what is foolish in the world to shame the wise; God chose what is weak in the world to shame the strong" (1 Corinthians 1:26–27).

Review 25:24–27.

9. Why had Festus gathered this group together?

Honestly, the situation was almost comical at this point. Five times in today's passage, Festus shared how he was at a total loss for why Paul was there.

10. Find the five verses, and list their references below.

The scene ended today with Festus priming Paul's audience for what they were about to hear. Many might've questioned why they were gathered for this spectacle. Based on Festus's setup, this seemed like a complete waste of everyone's time. But as we'll see in the coming days, Paul wasted no opportunity to bear witness for the Lord.

Acts 26:1–11

Begin today with a review of 25:23.

1. To get a visual of what took place, draw a courtroom sketch of the scene in the audience hall, including each person and group Luke named.

Review 26:1–5.

Paul began his defense by directly addressing King Agrippa.

2. What was Paul defending himself against?

"... against all the accusations __ ___ ____" (26:2).

Paul was standing before Roman officials, in a civil court, facing alleged civil crimes. The undertone of Paul's introduction seemed to be, "*This isn't about me breaking civil laws. I know it. You know it. They know it.*"

Remember, Agrippa was both Jewish and a Roman official. He understood the "customs and controversies of the Jews" (26:3). This was a good moment for Paul to point out that, as Agrippa already knew, some of these Jewish leaders were reactive and prone to exaggeration—Paul's case in point.

As we've seen before, Paul began by sharing his Jewish pedigree—a background Paul's accusers seemed to ignore. It was from his knowledge of the Scriptures that he had such confidence Jesus was the Messiah. Paul had put all his hope in Jesus as the promised one. For his Jewish accusers, that was precisely the problem.

Review 26:6-8.

3. Notice the repetition of this issue by filling in the blanks.

"And now I stand here on trial because of __ _____ __ ___ ______" (26:6)

". . . to which our twelve tribes _____ __ _______" (26:7)

"___ ___ ___ _____ I am accused by Jews, O king!" (26:7)

4. What "promise" was he referring to in 26:6?

Paul was on trial because he had found this hope. The promise had been fulfilled (Luke 4:21)! For generations, the Jews had studied the Scriptures. They "earnestly worship[ed] night and day" (26:7) with anticipation of the coming king, *and yet* their hearts were darkened to the truth that Jesus was the fulfillment of that promise.

5. What question did Paul ask his audience?

It should not have been shocking to the Jews that God raises the dead. Paul's accusers, so well-studied in the Scriptures, should have recognized Jesus as the Messiah in the clear signs pointing to Him from the Old Testament.

6. Compare the Old Testament prophecies with their corresponding New Testament passages below, and record how Jesus was the fulfillment of each.

Old Testament	New Testament	Fulfillment
Psalm 22:16	Luke 24:39	
Isaiah 53:12	Mark 15:27	
Psalm 22:18	Matthew 27:35	

Paul also testified to this in his straightforward presentation of the gospel in 1 Corinthians 15.

7. Fill in the blanks.

> "For I delivered to you as of first importance what I also received: that Christ died for our sins ____________________________, that he was buried, that he was raised on the third day ____________________________" (1 Corinthians 15:3–4).

Since the fall of humankind, all of creation had been waiting for the restoration that came through the resurrection of Jesus. It was incredible to Paul that this was so incredible to them.

★ 8. How did such learned men become so blinded to the truth? How can you guard against this in your own life?

Review 26:9–11.

In a sense, Paul understood their thinking. Until his eyes had been opened, he'd stood exactly where his accusers were.

★ 9. List the ways Paul acted similarly toward Christians before his conversion.

Paul was not listing his Pharisaical accolades. You can almost hear sadness and regret in his voice. Jesus had warned His disciples about men like Paul: "They will put you out of the synagogues. Indeed, the hour is coming when whoever kills you will think he is offering service to God" (John 16:2).

Yes, that was who Paul had been—a raging, violent, zealous persecutor of the saints. But that was then. As he humbly described his dark past, he set his listeners up to hear one of the biggest plot twists in the New Testament. Despite the accusations against him, he knew this was a divine appointment.

DAY 5

Acts 26:12–32

 READ ACTS 26:12–32

Review 26:12–18.

This is the third time we've read Paul's story of conversion. Luke narrated the first instance in Acts 9, and Paul himself gave us the second and third accounts as he stood before the Jewish leaders and Roman officials. As with every other moment of suffering, beating, or imprisonment in the book of Acts, God had a purpose.

This was the end of Paul's trial in Caesarea before he was sent off to Rome. We might think he would use this moment to plead his case to the king and make a last-ditch effort to be set free. However, not once in this speech did Paul ask for pardon. Instead, he discerned the spiritual opportunity before him and chose to speak words of life to the men and women listening.

1. According to the words of Jesus here, how does one receive forgiveness of sins and a place among those who are sanctified?

Paul explained to his audience a truth he had been blinded to his entire life—that is, until Jesus struck him with blindness to help him see. After he saw the light (literally), his one purpose in life was to open others' eyes to see that salvation comes by faith in Christ alone.

★ 2. Are you sometimes inclined to think there is more you must do to receive a place among the sanctified?

Review 26:19–32.

Despite his past, Paul had been used by God to take the gospel to Damascus, to Jerusalem, and all throughout the region of Judea. And now, even as a captive, he had a captive audience in a group of Roman officials.

3. What sustained Paul during all his trials and suffering?

★ 4. What does this tell you about the goodness and sovereignty of God? How does that encourage you in your current circumstances?

When we share the gospel, there are core elements our message should always include: repentance of sin, Christ's suffering and dying for our sins, and Jesus's resurrection.

5. List the two verses where we see this gospel outline in Paul's discourse.

While Paul was still speaking, Festus dismissively accused Paul of being insane. He was so astounded at Paul's message and knowledge that he knew he couldn't debate him. But notice who had not yet chimed in: Agrippa. As we've seen previously, the Holy Spirit seemed to give Paul insight into spiritual matters. It's possible Paul sensed a stirring in Agrippa at this moment, so he dug in.

6. When Paul asked Agrippa if he believed, how did Agrippa respond?

A. "Yes! Tell me more!"

B. "No, I think you're insane too."

C. He avoided it by answering the question with a question.

In 26:29, Paul revealed his hope for every person in his hearing. At this point, Paul had stood before High Priest Ananias, Governor Felix, Governor Festus, and King Agrippa. We have discussed ad nauseam the charges against him, the lack of proof, and the political chess match in which Paul seemed a pawn . . . but was he? Perhaps we find our answer tucked in the prophetic call the Lord placed on Paul's life on a street called Straight (9:11, 15).

7. Write 9:15 below and circle the three audiences Jesus said He would send Paul to.

Agrippa's statement at the end of the chapter might make us think Paul had chosen unwisely when he appealed to Caesar Nero. But his appeal led to the fulfillment of 23:11.

8. Fill in the blank in 23:11 below.

> "Take courage, for as you have testified to the facts about me in Jerusalem, so you must testify also in ______."

Under the sovereign hand of God, Paul was man's pawn. He was God's chosen instrument for this very purpose. Men like Festus, who may have never heard the name of Jesus, heard the gospel from the lips of a renowned prisoner. While Paul may have been bound in chains, he stood freer than any of his accusers and invited them to join him in the Way.

9. Is there a specific circumstance or relationship where you feel stuck? Does it sometimes feel like your life lacks purpose? What encouragement can you glean from Paul's story?

Remember, as a child of God, you are His chosen instrument, part of His sovereign plan for reaching the lost in the name of Jesus. Invite those you know to join the Way. Share with them that He's where the joy is!

10. What stood out to you most in this week's study? Why?

11. What did you learn or relearn about God and His character this week?

DAY 6

Corresponding Psalm & Prayer

READ PSALM 3

1. What correlation do you see between Psalm 3 and this week's study?

2. What portions of this psalm stand out to you most?

3. Close by praying this prayer aloud:

Father,

You are above all others on Your holy hill, and still You answer me. When I'm in darkness, You lift my head. When I'm surrounded by enemies, You're my shield. I sleep because You give me peace. I wake because You sustain me. No matter what may come, I know You will deliver me. Like Paul, I have the help that comes from You.

Yet even though I know I'm in Your hands, I've looked elsewhere for comfort. I've tried—and failed—to add to my salvation. I've done good things with wrong motives. Forgive me. Remind me again that You alone give salvation.

I've sought—and sometimes found—others' approval, even when it meant ignoring Your commands. I've gained favor in their eyes at the cost of my conscience. Forgive me. Remind me that one day I will stand before You and the approval of the world will mean nothing.

I surrender my life to You, Lord—every moment of my day, each decision I make, I yield my will and way to Your perfect will and way.

I love You too. Amen.

DAY 7

Rest, Catch Up, or Dig Deeper

WEEKLY CHALLENGE

Despite years of standing on trial and sitting in jail, Paul remained consistent and steadfast in his God-given purpose. He was certain of his calling and the commission God had given him to take light to the Gentiles. He met people almost every day who had never even heard the name of Jesus, which served as a reminder to use every opportunity to boldly share the gospel.

Using Paul's life as an example, remind yourself each day of *your* commission. Ask God to give you His perspective of the world around you and the circumstances in which He has placed you. This week, you may have an opportunity to stand before leaders and represent Christ. Or you may have normal, seemingly monotonous days. But where in that monotony is God commissioning you for His kingdom? Look for it. Pray for it. Act on it.

WEEK 10

Acts 27–28

Approximate Years: AD 60–62

Scripture to Memorize

And the believers from among the circumcised who had come with Peter were amazed, because the gift of the Holy Spirit was poured out even on the Gentiles.

Acts 10:45

DAILY BIBLE READING

Day 1: Acts 27:1–12
Day 2: Acts 27:13–38
Day 3: Acts 27:39–44
Day 4: Acts 28:1–16
Day 5: Acts 28:17–31
Day 6: Psalm 89
Day 7: Catch-Up Day

Corresponds to Day 348 of *The Bible Recap*.

WEEKLY CHALLENGE

See page 265 for more information.

DAY 1

Acts 27:1–12

 **READ ACTS 27:1–12**

With impressive detail, Luke chronicled his and Paul's nightmare of a journey across the Mediterranean. (Yep, Luke was still with Paul on the journey to Rome. Did you notice his use of *we* in today's reading?)

1. Update your timeline (page 19) to record that in the year 60, Paul and Luke's journey to Rome began.

Review 27:1–8.

Paul and other prisoners were delivered to Julius, their new centurion. A Roman centurion commanded one hundred soldiers, and a cohort usually consisted of six to ten centurions and their soldiers. During prisoner transports, centurions were assigned to guard certain prisoners. The job could be dangerous, but it paid well—about five times a soldier's salary.[1]

★ 2. How did Julius treat Paul? Can you think of another experience Paul had that was similar? What does this reveal about God's heart?

The journey did not start smoothly. The crew fought the winds by sailing "under the lee" (27:4)—or right beside the coastline—to Myra. There, they switched to a larger ship that was probably transporting grain.[2]

3. **Do a web search for a first-century Roman grain ship.** Write or draw what you learn about it below.

Though this ship was larger and better equipped than the first, it was essentially still a sailboat, at the mercy of the wind and the waves.

4. On the map below, trace the route the group intended to take from Myra to Rome. Then find and circle Fair Havens, a stop on their actual route.

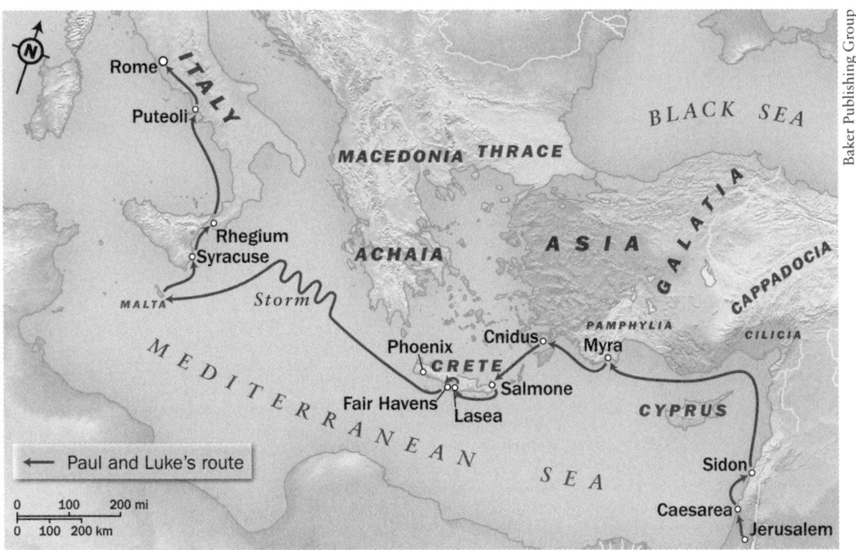

Baker Publishing Group

The ship was off course as soon as they left Myra. The usual route to Rome would've taken them north of Crete. But because of the strong winds, they wound up south of the island.

Review 27:9–10.

By the time the crew made it to the small port town of Fair Havens, the Fast was over.

5. **Use a Greek lexicon to fill in the table below.**

	The Fast
What was it?	
On what day was it observed every year?	
At what time of year was it observed?	

It's interesting to note that Luke referred to this day as "the Fast" instead of "the Day of Atonement."

6. **Read Leviticus 23:27–28.** What happened on the Day of Atonement?

In the Old Testament, once a year, the high priest sacrificed a goat to atone for the sins of the people. That annual sacrifice wasn't needed anymore. Jesus, the ultimate High Priest, was Himself the once-and-for-all-time sacrificial Lamb. But given that Luke acknowledges the day by calling it "the Fast," it seems that he and Paul (and possibly other Jewish believers) may have wanted to honor God by observing that portion of the holiday.

The fact that the Fast had already occurred meant it was late fall. So for these sailors and passengers, the journey was going to be *rough*. In the fall and winter, Mediterranean weather is volatile. Sudden storms are common, accompanied by choppy waters. Even when it's not storming, cloud cover is often total. Roman sailors used the night sky to navigate their journeys, so if they couldn't see the stars, they couldn't navigate.

Even today, on modern ships equipped with state-of-the-art navigation tools, far fewer cruises sail through the Mediterranean in the fall and winter than in the spring and summer. And if you book an off-season cruise, some tour companies will warn you ahead of time of the potential for unpredictable weather and unpleasant passage through open water.

Review 27:11–12.

Since it was dangerous to sail any farther, Paul warned everyone they should stay put. In 27:11, we learn that the centurion heard Paul but—perhaps because he wasn't yet sure what to make of his prisoner—paid more attention to the ship's owner and the pilot (captain). They wanted to reach the larger port city of Phoenix and spend the winter there.

★ 7. What reasons could have motivated the pilot and ship owner to risk the journey to Phoenix? **Use a study tool for help.**

Even though Paul's words to the crew might not have been divinely inspired, it's clear he understood the weather patterns of the Mediterranean and had some common sense. He knew this journey was a bad idea. Paul made an appeal for the leaders to come to their senses and abandon their folly. But unfortunately for them all, that ship had sailed.

DAY 2

Acts 27:13–38

Review 27:13–14.

As the crew sailed again, a gentle wind blew them in the right direction, and for a short while, it probably seemed like everything was looking up. But suddenly—as is common in the late fall on the Mediterranean—a violent northeastern wind blew in.

If you live on the east coast of Canada or the northern United States, you're probably familiar with the wild and unpredictable gusts of nor'easters; these are the same type of winds. Today in the Mediterranean, these cold winds are called *tramontane*, and they often bring lengthy storms. There's an Italian expression—*perdere la tramontana*—that essentially means "to lose the way."[1] And that's exactly what happened to Paul and Luke's ship.

Review 27:15–19.

1. Complete the storyboard below, using Luke's account of the next few days.

Draw a picture						
Fill in the caption	They had to undergird the ship, most likely tying it together with ropes.		On the second day, they tossed cargo over.			After days of the storm and losing their way, most had lost hope.
Cite the reference		27:17		27:19	27:20	

Review 27:21–26.

While it's safe to say no one was having a pleasant journey, one of the passengers—more specifically, one of the prisoners—hadn't lost hope. After an *I told you so* moment, Paul spoke to the passengers and crew, proving his wisdom, establishing his authority, and encouraging them.

★ 2. **Reread Paul's speech from 27:21–26, then complete the table below.** You can paraphrase or quote directly from the text.

Which parts of Paul's message . . .

proved his wisdom?	established his authority?	encouraged the crew and passengers?

Paul was confident in the message God had given him, and he knew they were all going to arrive safely on land. But safe arrival wasn't immediate, and the wind and the waves kept raging. For two weeks, the ship was at the mercy of a ruthless storm, and the passengers could do nothing but wait it out.

3. Have you had to "wait it out" during a time of suffering? How was your faith impacted?

Review 27:27–32.

On the fourteenth night, the storm had driven the ship to the Adriatic Sea, which extended farther south at that time than it does today. The sailors thought they were finally nearing land. Their measurements told them they were correct: The water was quickly becoming shallower. Once the depth of the sea under the ship was fifteen fathoms (about ninety feet), they dropped four anchors and prayed for daylight to come.

Feeling better about the fate of a dinghy than their tied-together ship of nightmares, some of the sailors attempted—but failed—to leave everyone else behind. Paul told the centurions that their lives depended on *everyone* staying on board, so the soldiers cut the ropes and the would-be lifeboat floated away.

Review 27:33–38.

★ 4. What did Paul do after taking bread and before eating it? How did the people on board respond? What does that teach us?

DAY 3

Acts 27:39–44

READ ACTS 27:39–44

Review 27:39–41.

After the ship's passengers and crew prayed, daylight arrived, and they finally saw land! No one recognized the beach, but they decided to run the ship onto it. They cast the four anchors off and left them in the sea, sailing toward the beach.

1. What happened next?

The ship struck ________

The ship's bow ________

The ship's stern ________

Just like Paul had warned them, the ship wrecked. We'll read tomorrow that the beach they were aiming for was on an island named Malta. On the northeast coast of Malta, there is an area that now is called St. Paul's Bay. Archaeologists have discovered ruins of first-century Roman roads and baths there, which means it was likely an important harbor city at the time of this shipwreck. If you visit St. Paul's Bay today, you'll see an ornate cathedral—creatively named St. Paul's Shipwreck Church—that was built there in the 1500s. For centuries, St. Paul's Bay was the agreed-upon site of this shipwreck.

But in the early 2000s, a former Los Angeles crime scene investigator visited St. Paul's Bay and realized that the biblical evidence didn't match the site he saw.

2. **Using Luke's thorough account of the location in 27:28–41, check all of the details that must be true about the shipwreck site.**

- ☐ There is a bay with a beach visible from the site.
- ☐ It's off the northeast coast of Malta.
- ☐ There's a reef or sandbar.
- ☐ The sea is about ninety feet deep at the site.
- ☐ The sailors knew the harbor well since they'd stopped there before.
- ☐ The sailors didn't recognize the area.

To the investigator, St. Paul's Bay didn't seem to match the information in Luke's account. So he hired groups of Maltese fishermen to take him to other bays around the island. The area he believed matched Luke's description most closely was on the southeast corner of the island, called St. Thomas Bay. Then one day, he met a fisherman who told him that in the 1960s, they'd found four ancient anchors in that bay, at a depth of about ninety feet. The anchors are in the Maritime Museum in Malta and have been confirmed to be first-century Roman anchors.[1]

We don't know for certain whether these anchors are *the* anchors or whether this bay is *the* bay, but we do know this: Every single word in the Bible is true. So if the four Roman anchors in the Maritime Museum weren't the anchors on Paul and Luke's ship, there were still four anchors. And if St. Thomas Bay isn't the bay where the ship wrecked, then the ship wrecked in another Maltese bay. The anchors existed. The bay existed. And the ship wrecked, just like an angel of God said it would.

Review 27:42–44.

3. Answer the following questions to set the scene.

Question	Answer	Reference
How many people were on the ship?		27:37
How long did the storm last?		27:27
How had the boat been held together during that time?		27:17
How often had they eaten during that time?		27:33
What was the state of the boat now?		27:41
What was the sea like in the bay?		27:41

It's an understatement to say the scene was chaotic. And as we've talked about before, the punishment for a Roman officer whose prisoners escaped was death. Keeping all of that in mind, it's almost understandable that the panicked soldiers' plan was to kill the prisoners before getting themselves to safety. (Re)enter: the centurion, Julius.

★ 4. What did Julius want? What did Julius do?

Just like He promised, God brought every single person on that ship safely to shore.

5. What does this tell you about who God is?

DAY 4

Acts 28:1–16

READ ACTS 28:1–16

Ships sailing from Myra to Rome often stopped on the island of Malta—though likely in a different city. Not only did God deliver the passengers from the storm, but He delivered them to a place where they were treated kindly. And He even put them back on course. Paul's trials weren't over yet, though; there would be many more hardships to come. Up first: a venomous snake.

Review 28:1–4.

When the viper attached itself to Paul's hand, the Maltese people thought their goddess was ensuring justice for crimes he'd committed. They decided Paul must have been a murderer. And he was. But while the people thought their goddess wanted him to die because of his sins, Paul knew the one true God died in his place to atone for his sins.

Review 28:5–6.

1. Describe the change in mindset of the Maltese people in just a few verses.

- They thought he was a _____ (28:4).
- They thought he was a _____ (28:6).

2. What does that reveal about human nature?

Review 28:7–9.

Based on his symptoms, Publius's father likely had a disease caused by bacteria in goat's milk. It was common at the time in the Mediterranean,[1] but could also be deadly. Paul healed the man with God-given power, and it wasn't long before the rest of the Maltese people who were afflicted with diseases came for healing too.

Review 28:10–11.

3. What happened after the winter was over?

A. Paul helped them build a church.
B. The Maltese people gave the crew and passengers everything they needed for the rest of their journey.
C. The Maltese people invited Paul to stay longer.
D. They rebuilt the ship together.

The people of Malta were generous toward physical needs, but God was generous toward them with something even greater. Church history tells us Paul is credited with bringing Christianity to Malta. The church that was planted there grew exponentially over generations. Today, Malta has one of the highest percentages of practicing Christians in the world: about 98 percent of the population. Despite everything Paul and Luke went through, God brought them safely to the island, where He showed His kindness not just to the ship's passengers, but also to the Maltese people.

Review 28:12–16.

After a few pit stops, Paul finally reached Rome, just as God said he would.

4. Update your timeline (page 19) to record that Paul arrived in Rome in the year 61.

5. According to 28:13–15, where did the brothers they met along the way come from? What does that tell you about the spread of the early church? How did seeing them impact Paul?

Before they arrived in Rome, Paul had already sent a letter to the Roman Christians. In that letter, he wrote, "We know that for those who love God all things work together for good, for those who are called according to his purpose" (Romans 8:28).

Can you imagine the joy and encouragement Paul must have felt when he reunited with his colaborers for the gospel? Though he'd come to Rome as a prisoner, Paul was confident in God's sovereignty and in His goodness.

★ 6. What are some of the ways God worked all things together for good in Paul's life?

★ 7. What are some of the ways God has worked all things together for good in your life?

DAY 5

Acts 28:17–31

READ ACTS 28:17–31

In Rome, Paul was a prisoner awaiting trial, but with remarkable freedoms. He was allowed to choose his housing and had many guests visit him. The first guests Paul sent for were not a surprising choice, given his methods in every city he visited.

Review 28:17–24.

1. Fill in the table below to review what happened next.

Question	Answer	Reference
Who visited Paul first?		28:17
Why was Paul sent to Rome?		28:17–19
Why was Paul really in captivity?		28:20
What did the leaders know about him?		28:21
What did the leaders know about "this sect" (the Way)?		28:22
When the larger group of leaders returned, what did Paul tell them?		28:23
How long did Paul testify to them?		28:23
What was the result of Paul's message?		28:24

Review 28:25–28. (Or 28:25–29 if your Bible includes it. Like 24:7, some early manuscripts excluded 28:29, so some modern translations exclude it as well.)

2. Fill in the prophecy Paul quoted in 28:27.

"For this people's _____ has grown _____, and with their _____ they can _____ _____, and their _____ they have _________."

In ancient Jewish culture, the "heart" wasn't only the center of affection but also the center of thought. Paul was saying the disbelieving leaders had closed off not only their hearts to love, but also their minds to truth. But Paul pointed out that Isaiah's prophecy meant the disbelieving leaders had been a part of God's plan all along: Salvation was for the Gentiles too!

Review 28:30–31.

3. Update your timeline (page 19) to note the final summary update on the growth of the church that was recorded in 28:31.

In Acts's final summary update on the growth of the church, we learn that Paul welcomed everyone who visited him, "proclaiming the kingdom of God and teaching about the Lord Jesus Christ with all boldness and without hindrance" (28:31).

In addition to teaching, Paul wrote letters during his time in Rome. The letters he wrote to the churches at Ephesus, Colossae, and Philippi were most likely written during this period. Luke didn't record what Paul taught the people who visited him, but because of his letters, we do have some insight into what was on Paul's heart at the time.

★ 4. Look up the following passages and write a few notes about what Paul shared with the Christians in each of these places.

Ephesians 2:1–9	Philippians 1:19–26	Colossians 3:1–17

★ 5. Now write in your own words how Paul might have "proclaimed the kingdom of God and taught about the Lord Jesus Christ" to his guests.

After Paul started following Jesus, he was attacked by mobs, run out of town, stoned, left for dead, imprisoned, run out of another town, arrested, tried, imprisoned again, shipwrecked, bitten by a viper, rejected, and put on house arrest. And there's still more to come for Paul.

Church history and clues in Scripture indicate Paul was probably released after two years in Rome, at which time he went on another missionary journey. He was later imprisoned again in Rome (and that time, under harsh conditions). He was deserted by many of his friends, and ultimately, he was martyred.

And yet through all of that, he wrote, "But whatever gain I had, I counted as loss for the sake of Christ. Indeed, I count everything as loss because of the surpassing worth of knowing Christ Jesus my Lord. For his sake I have suffered the loss of all things and count them as rubbish, in order that I may gain Christ and be found in him" (Philippians 3:7–9).

Despite everything he went through, Paul—and so many others throughout church history—never lost sight of the incomparable beauty of Christ. In his letter to the Ephesians, Paul encouraged husbands to love their wives, just as Jesus "loved the church and gave himself up for her" (Ephesians 5:25). As part of the global church, we are the bride, waiting for our Bridegroom to return. At the end of this age, there will be a wedding ceremony, and all things will be made new (Revelation 21:1–5).

Nothing compares to Jesus. He's the Savior who died so we could live. He's the God who defeated the grave. He's the one who poured out the Spirit on believers. He's the Bridegroom of the church. And He's where the joy is!

6. What stood out to you most in this week's study? Why?

7. What did you learn or relearn about God and His character this week?

DAY 6

Corresponding Psalm & Prayer

READ PSALM 89

1. What correlation do you see between Psalm 89 and this week's study?

2. What portions of this psalm stand out to you most?

3. Close by praying this prayer aloud:

Father,

Let everything in the heavens and on the earth praise You! Let us sing of Your steadfast love and make known Your faithfulness to all generations. Your church hears the call to worship, and we're blessed to sing of Your righteousness!

You rule the raging sea and calm the rising waves. But I am tossed by ripples in still water. You crush Your enemies with Your mighty hand. But I cower at rejection, even at a mere dismissal. You give Your people an exalted place, above everything else You created. But I have doubted Your goodness, Your care for me, and Your promises.

Remind me who You are and who I am. Teach me to sing the song of Your steadfast love all the days of my life.

I surrender my life to You, Lord—every moment of my day, each decision I make, I yield my will and way to Your perfect will and way.

I love You too. Amen.

DAY 7

Rest, Catch Up, or Dig Deeper

WEEKLY CHALLENGE

The early church was marked by unity, having "all things in common" (Acts 2:44). Throughout Acts, as the gospel spread and the church grew, it included people who had seemingly nothing in common. They were from different regions, spoke different languages, came from different cultures, and had varying levels of education and wealth. Some were men; some were women. Some were Jews; some were Gentiles. The unifying factor was Christ.

Visit a church that faithfully preaches the gospel of Jesus and that has different traditions from your own church. Pray for a spirit of unity as you attend, and look for the things you have in common with those brothers and sisters. As a bonus challenge, after visiting, write the pastor or ministers a letter encouraging them in their work building God's church.

FOR GROUP LEADERS

Thank you for using this study and leading others through it as well! Each week has a wide variety of content (daily Bible reading, content and questions, Scripture memorization, weekly challenge, and resources) to help the reader develop a range of spiritual disciplines. Feel free to include as much or as little of that in your meetings as you'd like. The details provided in How to Use This Study (pp. 11–13) will be helpful to you and all your group members, so be sure to review that information together!

It's up to you and your group how you'd like to structure your meetings, but we suggest including time for discussion of the week's study and Bible text, mutual encouragement, and prayer. You may also want to practice your Scripture memory verses together as a group or in pairs. As you share with each other, "consider how to stir up one another to love and good works" (Hebrews 10:24) and "encourage one another and build one another up" (1 Thessalonians 5:11).

Here are some sample questions to help facilitate discussion. This is structured as a weekly study, but if your group meets at a different frequency, you may wish to adjust the questions accordingly. Cover as many questions as time allows, or feel free to come up with your own. And don't forget to check out the additional resources we've linked for you at MyDGroup.org/Resources/Acts.

Sample Discussion Questions

What questions did this week's study or Bible text bring up for you?

What stood out to you in this week's study?

What did you notice about God and His character?

How were you challenged by your study of the Bible text? Is there anything you want to change in light of what you learned?

How does what you learned about God affect the way you live in community?

What correlation did you see between the psalm from Day 6 and this week's study of Acts?

Have you felt God working in you through the weekly challenge? If so, how?

Is your love for God's Word increasing as we go through this study? If so, how?

Did anything you learned increase your joy in knowing Jesus?

ACKNOWLEDGMENTS

Olivia Le, who sets us up for success with all our writing summits!

Bonnie Hartwig, who took over the role of house mom and proved once again that she does nothing halfway. The signs! The spread! What a gift!

Laura Buchelt, who championed us through this study and smoothed over all our rough edges.

Emily Pickell, who is steady and unflappable, always bringing rich insights and wisdom.

Liz Suggs, who adapts—like the pro that she is—to all our nuanced writing needs.

Abbey Dane, who didn't know she was auditioning for a full-time job but passed the test with flying colors!

Kirsten McCloskey, whose mind for attention to theological detail is a blessing to every reader.

Lisa Jackson—our forest guide and friend, bringing beauty, courage, light, and truth into every new and scary step.

Rich Jackson, who is the unsung hero of all our writing summits. Without you we would surely all be eaten by bears.

Jeff Braun, Hannah Ahlfield, and Stephanie Smith, who somehow manage to not only keep us on pace, but keep us smiling (and help us be as accurate as possible) in the process!

Notes

Week 4: Day 5

1. John Foxe, *Foxe's Book of Martyrs* (Philadelphia: Charles Foster Publishing Co., 1895), 27.

Week 7: Day 1

1. David Guzik, "Acts 18 – Paul in Corinth; the End of the Second Missionary Journey and Beginning of the Third," 2018, https://enduringword.com/bible-commentary/acts-18/.
2. David Guzik, "Study Guide for Acts 18 by David Guzik," Blue Letter Bible, last modified June 2022, https://www.blueletterbible.org/comm/guzik_david/study-guide/acts/acts-18.cfm.

Week 7: Day 2

1. David Guzik, "Study Guide for Acts 19 by David Guzik," Blue Letter Bible, last modified June 2022, https://www.blueletterbible.org/comm/guzik_david/study-guide/acts/acts-19.cfm.

Week 7: Day 4

1. David Guzik, "Study Guide for Acts 20 by David Guzik," Blue Letter Bible, last modified June 2022, https://www.blueletterbible.org/comm/guzik_david/study-guide/acts/acts-20.cfm.

Week 9: Day 2

1. A. N. Sherwin-White, *Roman Society and Roman Law in the New Testament: The Sarum Lectures 1960–1961* (Eugene, OR: Wipf & Stock Publishers, 1963), 58–59.

Week 10: Day 1

1. *ESV Women's Study Bible* (Crossway, 2020), 1775n10:1.
2. *ESV Women's Study Bible* (Crossway, 2020), 1813n27:6.

Week 10: Day 2

1. *Cambridge Dictionary*, "tramontana," accessed September 27, 2024, https://dictionary.cambridge.org/dictionary/italian-english/tramontana.

Week 10: Day 3

1. Chuck Holton, "Searching for Paul's Shipwreck on Malta," CBN, January 30, 2015, https://www2.cbn.com/news/world/searching-pauls-shipwreck-malta.

Week 10: Day 4

1. Tremper Longman III and David E. Garland, eds., *The Expositor's Bible Commentary: Luke–Acts*, Vol. 10, rev. ed. (Grand Rapids, MI: Zondervan, 2007), 1091.

ABOUT THE EDITOR

TARA-LEIGH COBBLE'S zeal for biblical literacy led her to create a network of Bible studies called D-Group International (Discipleship Group). Every week, hundreds of men's and women's D-Groups meet in homes, in churches, and online for Bible study and accountability.

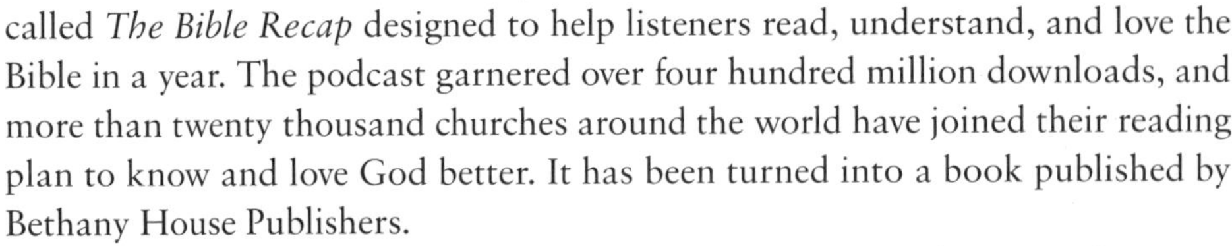

She also writes and hosts a daily podcast called *The Bible Recap* designed to help listeners read, understand, and love the Bible in a year. The podcast garnered over four hundred million downloads, and more than twenty thousand churches around the world have joined their reading plan to know and love God better. It has been turned into a book published by Bethany House Publishers.

Tara-Leigh is a *Wall Street Journal* bestselling author, speaks to a wide variety of audiences, and regularly leads teaching trips to Israel because she loves to watch others be awed by the story of Scripture through firsthand experience.

Her favorite things include sparkling water and days that are 72 degrees with 55 percent humidity, and she thinks every meal tastes better when eaten outside. She lives in a concrete box in the skies of Dallas, Texas, where she has no pets, children, or anything that might die if she forgets to feed it.

For more information about Tara-Leigh and her ministries, you can visit her online.

Websites: taraleighcobble.com | thebiblerecap.com | mydgroup.org | israelux.com
Social media: @taraleighcobble | @thebiblerecap | @mydgroup | @israeluxtours